THE TEMPEST

THE TEMPEST

William Shakespeare

Edited by
CEDRIC WATTS

WORDSWORTH CLASSICS

For my husband
ANTHONY JOHN RANSON
with love from your wife, the publisher.
Eternally grateful for your unconditional love.

Readers who are interested in other titles from
Wordsworth Editions are invited to visit our website at
www.wordsworth-editions.com

First published in 1994 by Wordsworth Editions Limited
8B East Street, Ware, Hertfordshire SG12 9HJ

ISBN 978 1 85326 203 6

Text © Wordsworth Editions Limited 2004
Introduction, notes and other editorial matter © Cedric Watts 2004

Wordsworth® is a registered trademark of
Wordsworth Editions Limited

Wordsworth Editions
is the company founded in 1987 by
MICHAEL TRAYLER

Typeset in Great Britain by Antony Gray
Printed and bound in Great Britain by Clays Ltd, Elcograf S.p.A.

CONTENTS

GENERAL INTRODUCTION

The Wordsworth Classics' Shakespeare Series, with *Romeo and Juliet, Henry V* and *The Merchant of Venice* as its inaugural volumes, presents a newly-edited sequence of William Shakespeare's works. Wordsworth Classics are inexpensive paperbacks for students and for the general reader. Each play in the Shakespeare Series is accompanied by a standard apparatus, including an introduction, explanatory notes and a glossary. The textual editing takes account of recent scholarship while giving the material a careful reappraisal. The apparatus is, however, concise rather than elaborate. We hope that the resultant volumes prove to be handy, reliable and helpful. Above all, we hope that, from Shakespeare's works, readers will derive pleasure, wisdom, provocation, challenges, and insights: insights into his culture and ours, and into the era of civilisation to which his writings have made – and continue to make – such potently influential contributions. Shakespeare's eloquence will, undoubtedly, re-echo 'in states unborn and accents yet unknown'.

CEDRIC WATTS
Series Editor

INTRODUCTION

'Imaginary gardens with real toads in them.' [1]

Around 1610, as Shakespeare's great sequence of tragedies came to its end, there emerged a distinctive group of late comedies which has been termed 'the romances'. These late works were: *Pericles* (which is largely though not wholly by Shakespeare), *Cymbeline*, *The Winter's Tale* and, finally, *The Tempest*. Since the seventeenth century, that term 'romances' has been applied to literary works which, in contrast to more realistic writings, offer the far-fetched, strange, peculiar and exotic; often they invoke the supernatural.[2] These plays fit the definition well. We move in unfamiliar times or regions; the magical and supernatural are prominent; events defy everyday logic; bizarre catastrophes are offset by apparent miracles. Although weak productions of these dramas can make parts of them seem ludicrous and preposterous, good productions can create a sense of mythical resonance, poignancy and profundity. We may find ourselves ambushed by emotion and startled by intuitive recognition.

A technical problem faced by Shakespeare in those four romances is the accommodation of two separate chronological periods, so that in the plot a 'time-gap' (of between twelve and twenty years) is evident. If we ask why there is a need for so lengthy an interim, the answer is thematic. Such a time-gap permits innocent children, representing new hope for the future, to become old enough to fall in love, marry and procreate. Their loving harmony compensates for the hateful discords of the past; and their virtue can be dynamic, continuing into the future and perhaps in their offspring. The passage of time is thus generational, generative and regenerative.

Characteristically in these four late plays, we begin with a world which appears to be tragic: we are shown jealousy, corruption, destruction, storms, suffering, death or apparent death. Eventually, by magic or as if by magic, the supposedly dead (or most of them) are found to be alive after all; and those people whose experience of suffering and loss has induced penitence are, unexpectedly and joyfully, reunited with those whom they had supposed gone for ever. Suffering, penitence, atonement, restoration, reconciliation and marriage are thematic preoccupations of these romances. This quartet of plays completes the pattern of Shakespeare's development as a dramatist: they are the post-tragic coda to his career. After immersion in the realm of tragedy, in which, though there may be therapeutic suffering, there is final emphasis on loss and destruction, what better imaginative transition than to a realm in which, after losses have induced some wisdom, the losses are made good, and the apparently dead are eventually resurrected here on earth?

In *Pericles*, there is a gap of more than thirteen years before Pericles can be reunited with his long-lost daughter and, later, with his wife (who had supposedly died at sea and was cast to the waves). In the sub-plot of *Cymbeline*, roughly twenty years elapse before Cymbeline is reunited with his long-lost sons, Guiderius and Arviragus. *The Winter's Tale* offers an interval specified as both fifteen and sixteen years, after which Leontes is reunited with his daughter, Perdita, and his wife, Hermione, both of whom he had thought dead. In *The Tempest*, twelve years elapse between the time when Prospero and his daughter were abandoned to the sea and the present action on the island when Miranda, whose age is now about fourteen, is old enough to become betrothed to Ferdinand. There were two ways in which Shakespeare could deal with the technical problem generated by the thematically-necessary interval of time. One way was obvious and linear: to depict the past corruption, then to declare a time-gap, and finally to depict the newer phase of discovery and recovery. Such was the way of *Pericles* and *The Winter's Tale*. In the former, the choric figure of Gower enters to usher us across the passing years. In the latter, 'Time, the Chorus' himself appears at the start of Act 4 to do the same job. (Shakespeare's contemporary, Ben Jonson, derided such devices, which he deemed clumsy and unrealistic.) [3] The second way of dealing with the problem was, obviously, to begin the action on the later side of the gap, employing retrospective narration to explain what had happened before it. So, in *Cymbeline*, a soliloquy by Belarius explains that many years previously he had kidnapped the young princes and that he has, since then, raised them as his sons in the wilds. In *The Tempest*, Prospero informs Miranda about the events that brought them to the island. This method ensures greater structural tidiness, though it does generate fresh problems. Prospero's retrospective speech is very long, and raises questions of realism: why had he not explained such matters long before? Miranda's own responses are inconsistent. She says: 'More to know / Did never meddle with my thoughts': in other words, she had never sought to know about the events prior to the island-life. A few lines later, however, she says that Prospero had often left her to 'a bootless inquisition': he had often failed to satisfy her curiosity. (The former response explains her present ignorance; the latter response provides a cue for Prospero's narration. Her inconsistency is plot-generated.)

To deal with the time-gap by means of a retrospective account certainly helps to make *The Tempest* structurally tidier than *The Winter's Tale*, though we pay a certain price for such tidiness. The latter play gives a stronger sense of destructive corruption, of bitter loss and the process of ageing. Nevertheless, after the sprawling, widely-dispersed action of *The Winter's Tale*, which roams across the decades and travels from Sicilia to Bohemia and back again, there is an impressive elegance and compactness to *The Tempest*. At times it brings to mind the famous neo-classical 'Unities' of action, place and time. Occasionally these have been wrongly attributed to Aristotle's *Poetics*; but Aristotle had emphasised only the need for a well-organised plot, and did not specify 'The Three Unities'; these were neo-classical conventions, influentially formulated by Lodovico Castelvetro in 1570.[4] Shakespeare approaches them reasonably closely. 'Unity of action' was the stipulation that any sub-plot should be either excluded or strongly integrated with the main plot. (Jean Racine, in such later plays as *Phèdre* and *Andromaque*, effectively met the stipulation.) In *The Tempest*, it may seem that the comic inter-action of Caliban, Stephano and Trinculo provides a diversionary sub-plot, and certainly it offers some farcical comic relief; but it proves to be integral with the main sequence. Caliban is Prospero's slave, and the comic trio plans to kill Prospero and take power. What's more, they are thus reprising, albeit in a farcical key, the plan of Antonio and Sebastian to kill Alonso so that Sebastian may become King of Naples; and, in a finely co-ordinating irony, Antonio cites as precedent of such an action his own supposedly successful act of usurpation against Prospero. This, in turn, helps to verify Prospero's narrative to Miranda and to give a stronger sense of the corruption that had prevailed on the mainland in the past. The theme of 'opposing the ruler' sounds throughout the play: it is expressed through Antonio (rebelling against his brother, the Duke), Sebastian (agreeing to conspire against his brother, the King), through Caliban, Stephano and Trinculo (in their futile plot against Prospero), briefly through Ferdinand (in his initial attempt to fight his captor), through Ariel (in his opposition to Sycorax, and in his quest for freedom from Prospero), and even, within the masque, through Venus and Cupid (in their plot to subvert the plans of Juno, Queen of the Olympians). In a minor key, the theme is present even in Prospero, to the extent that he is tempted to stray from the divine precept to be merciful.

Ancient drama treated locations flexibly: the action of Aeschylus's *Oresteia*, for instance, roams between Argos, Delphi and Athens. Accordingly, Aristotle did not commend any 'Unity of Place'; but this, too, emerged with neo-classicism in the late sixteenth century. Eventually, Racine (in his *Andromaque*) would reduce the dramatic location to one chamber in a palace, relying on reportage to deal with events outside it. Just how big the 'one place' of a drama should be was obviously open to debate; but, in contrast to the roaming action of *The Winter's Tale*, it is notable that the events of *The Tempest* are relatively localised: after the first scene, in which a vessel is wrecked on the island's coast, the action is confined to that island, and much of the time we are simply 'before Prospero's cell'. Indeed, confinement itself becomes another theme of the drama. Only at a unique time, when a particular star is in the ascendant, can Prospero's magic take effect; and, if all goes well, he may be able, at last, to escape from confinement on the island to the mainland of Italy. During the play, we are reminded that Ariel was once imprisoned in a cloven tree by Sycorax; and both Ariel and Caliban are held in the power of Prospero's magic. For a while, too, Alonso, Gonzalo, Sebastian, Antonio, Adrian and Francisco are all held paralysed within the enchanted circle inscribed on the ground by Prospero. The mariners are released after being 'clapped under hatches'. Alonso is eventually freed from the mental shackles of guilt and melancholy. Ariel is liberated, and Caliban can choose his own future. The theme resonates in the drama's epilogue, when the actor of Prospero pleads for the applause which will enable him to escape the confinement of the stage. The theatre itself is another 'enchanted circle' confining the audience during the performance.

The Tempest also approaches the neo-classical 'Unity of Time'. Aristotle had simply remarked that 'tragedy tries as far as possible to keep within a single revolution of the sun, or only slightly to exceed it'.[5] The neo-classical principle, however, was that the duration of the fictional time should be twelve hours at most, and ideally should approximate the real duration of time in the theatre. The plot of *The Tempest* unfolds between 2 p.m. and 6 p.m., and is twice specified as three hours (at 5.1.186 and 223). In the theatre, the length of the action varies considerably according to the nature of the production, but a matinée performance might well last from 2 p.m. to nearly 5 p.m. Among Shakespeare's plays, the two works which come nearest to being neo-classical in convention are *The Tempest*, his last play (if collaborative dramas be excluded), and one of the earliest plays, *The Comedy of Errors*. That early work has an action beginning in the morning and concluding in the evening of the same day. *The Comedy of Errors* is predominantly farcical: exuberantly expanding Plautus's *Menaechmi*, which exploited just one pair of identical twins, Shakespeare provides two pairs, multiplying the cases of mistaken identity. Nevertheless, to the brisk and lively central action, Shakespeare has added material taken from Gower's *Confessio Amantis*; and that material, in a curious anticipation of the late romances, deals with the sundering of a family at a time of storm at sea. Eventually, old Egeon is poignantly reunited not only with his lost sons but also with his wife, whom he believed to have died many years previously. The four romances, then, which so resonantly offer a post-tragic phase after a decade of great tragedies, have had a brief but telling anticipation in *The Comedy of Errors*, which may imaginatively have served as a post-tragic response to *Titus Andronicus*, Shakespeare's first tragedy.

In their metaphysical implications, the four romances offer a strange blend of the Christian, the classical, and, at times, modes of lyrical mysticism and scepticism. The Christian quality lies in the emphasis on the human capacity not only for sin but also for penitence and atonement, mercy being granted to the penitent. 'The rarer action is / In virtue than in vengeance', declares Prospero; and by 'virtue' he here means 'forgiveness'. Repeatedly, there are invocations with Christian implications: 'Heavens thank you', 'O the heavens!', cries Miranda; while Prospero asserts that 'Providence divine' had saved the two of them from the ocean. (We may recall the biblical stories of Noah, of Jonah, or of Jesus when he stilled the storm. The raising of Lazarus provides Christian precedent for the resurrection of an apparently dead person on earth.)

Classical theology describes a multiplicity of deities who not only rule mortals but also mingle with them; and those deities are often associated with the seasonal cycle and the bounty of nature. In *The Tempest*, spirits commanded by Prospero assume the rôles of Ceres, Iris and Juno: Ceres, the goddess of cereal crops, Iris, goddess of the rainbow, and Juno, goddess of marriage and procreation. The masque in which they appear helps to integrate the moral process of Prospero's plot with the benign aspects of nature, and thereby to provide a sensuous enrichment of the process so that it combines human and natural procreative forces. In any case, a play incorporating classical figures and dealing with modes of resurrection will remind us (and be enriched by memories) of such classical myths and legends of resurrection as those of Demeter and Persephone, of Admetus and Alcestis, or of Aphrodite and Adonis. Such material, if remote, is yet familiar, evoking the springtime rebirth of verdure and the perennial replacement of the older generation by the younger.

Early in the action of *The Tempest*, Prospero emphasises the contrast between the malign magic of Sycorax and his own benign magic. Nevertheless, to be a magician at all was then suspect and certainly perilous. One of the distinctive features of Prospero's character is a quality of sternness and even, at times, of harshness. His exile to the island bore a grain of justice, for his absorption in lonely studies had fostered Antonio's act of usurpation. Now, Prospero's attempt to punish his enemies and their companions runs the risk of becoming vindictive; and an important crux occurs when Ariel, in Act 5, scene 1, says:

> Your charm so strongly works 'em
> That, if you now beheld them, your affections
> Would become tender.

When Prospero says: 'Dost thou think so, spirit?', Ariel replies: 'Mine would sir, were I human.' Then Prospero responds with:

> And mine shall.
> Hast thou (which art but air) a touch, a feeling
> Of their afflictions, and shall not myself,
> One of their kind, that relish all as sharply
> Passion as they, be kindlier moved than thou art?
> Though with their high wrongs I am struck to th' quick,
> Yet, with my nobler reason, 'gainst my fury
> Do I take part . . .

Here a sprite, a thing of air, reminds Prospero of what it is to be truly human; and the play thereby is confirmed as a comedy rather than as a revenge drama. Nevertheless, the speech in which Prospero proclaims his decision to abandon his magic ('Ye elves of hills . . .': 5.1.33-57) reverberates with proud egotism. In that long invocation, the words 'I' and 'my' re-echo repeatedly, so that an actor may easily give him a tone of almost dictatorial harshness. Furthermore, Shakespeare's main source for that speech (which he found in Golding's translation of Ovid's *Metamorphoses*) was a declamation by Medea, the destructive enchantress; so the contrast between benign and malign magic is, for a while, eroded. Nevertheless, Prospero does indeed break his staff and drown his book. However gratifying the exercise of supernatural power, he will become a mere mortal among mortals; and, on the mainland, he will meditate on the death which awaits him: the death so poignantly invoked in the play's most moving speech. This comes when (in Act 4, scene 1) Prospero has abruptly dismissed the masque. Ferdinand looks dismayed, and Prospero says:

Our revels now are ended. These our actors
(As I foretold you) were all spirits, and
Are melted into air, into thin air;
And, like the baseless fabric of this vision,
The cloud-capped towers, the gorgeous palaces,
The solemn temples, the great globe itself,
Yea, all which it inherit, shall dissolve,
And, like this insubstantial pageant faded,
Leave not a rack behind. We are such stuff
As dreams are made on; and our little life
Is rounded with a sleep. Sir, I am vexed.

It's commonplace to say that nothing lasts for ever; but Prospero's way of expressing the idea transforms the commonplace into the visionary and profound. Prospero, explaining the disappearance of the masque, claims that such magical vanishing-tricks are quite natural, because we are all part of one cosmic vanishing-trick: lofty and splendid buildings must all evaporate, and our very planet must, in time, cease to exist. Indeed, the temporal seems to dissolve into the emptily spatial. As for human beings, they are as insubstantial as dreams, and, after the dream of life, we enter the sleep of death. He does not offer the traditional Christian consolation that we may enter eternal life in heaven. The emphasis is on evanescence, a fading away. He has exalted the status of his magic by demoting the status of the reality within which the magic operates. Perhaps that is another reason, apart from his recollection of the conspiracy, for his being vexed. The speech resonates outwards to the audience, for it suggests that theatrical illusion – and such illusions as The Tempest itself – may offer a paradigm of our temporary habitation of a dissolving world: a world which vanishes as each of us meets death.

The almost vertiginous interactions of reality and illusion, and the related sense of ambiguous transformations, extend from beginning to end of the play. The opening scene, in which the ship is beset by storm and starts to sink, seems graphically realistic; yet the next scene assures us that the manifest destruction was largely illusory. At the play's end, the Epilogue blurs the distinction between reality and illusion by letting the speaker be partly Prospero, partly the actor playing Prospero, and partly (to the ears of those who harbour biographical speculations) the author. Its last six lines, in which that voice not only prays for its hearers' indulgence but also, apparently, solicits their intercessionary prayers to God, the ultimate source of mercy, are certainly more earnest and devout, in tone and substance, than is customary in such an epilogue.[6] The ambiguous plea for applause may seem to imply a graver plea, and one which would be understandable in an era when the Puritans were quick to denounce playwrights and the world of the theatre. A playwright might well experience guilt: had not Shakespeare, in Sonnet 111, complained that 'almost thence my nature is subdued / To what it works in, like the dyer's hand'?

During the action of *The Tempest*, there are many transformations, some of which are ordained by Prospero, and some of which seems to exceed his range and to be inherent in the nature of the island. Caliban keenly registers that sense of fluid metamorphosis. He says:

> Be not afeard. The isle is full of noises,
> Sounds and sweet airs, that give delight, and hurt not:
> Sometimes a thousand twangling instruments
> Will hum about mine ears; and sometime voices,
> That, if I then had waked after long sleep,
> Will make me sleep again; and then, in dreaming,
> The clouds methought would open, and show riches
> Ready to drop upon me, that when I waked,
> I cried to dream again.

In its interfusion of waking-state and dreaming-state, it anticipates that noted speech of Prospero's beginning 'Our revels now are ended'; but whereas Prospero had invoked a dissolving away of all things into oblivion, Caliban invokes lyrically a cycle in which the delightful music and voices of the island induce sleep and dreams so splendid that even the waking delight seems less than the visionary dream-state. The closing words, 'I cried to dream again', will re-echo in the mind of any parent who has seen a baby waken from contented slumber and begin to wail; and they may even stir elusive recollections of our own infancy. In contrast to Prospero's vision of annihilating dissolution, Caliban evokes a sense of blissful interfusion.

This speech has helped to make Caliban one of the most para-doxical characterisations in Shakespeare's works. His very name is teasingly ambiguous. Some critics take it to be an anagram – however imperfect – of 'cannibal'; but that does not fit very well, given that Caliban's ideas of food (detailed in 2.2.161-6) are orthodox enough, and he expresses no desire to eat human flesh. Critics also suggest a derivation from 'Carib', an inhabitant of the Caribbean region; but this island is definitely located in the Mediterranean. Another possibility is that the name derives from the Romany word 'cauliban' (or 'kauloben'), meaning 'black'; [7] but, again, this is not a neat fit, for Caliban is not described as being black in hue. Nevertheless (in a moment to gratify Freudians), Prospero memorably says of him, 'This thing of darkness I/Acknowledge mine'. The case for Caliban as a 'thing of darkness' is clear enough. He is the offspring of a witch exiled from Algiers. His father, according to Prospero, was the devil; and, though this may be Prospero's slander, witches were reputed to have sexual relationships with Satan or with lesser devils. (Such diabolical figures were sometimes depicted with black faces.) Although initially treated kindly by Prospero and Miranda, Caliban has been surly, resentful, rebellious and vicious: he had once attempted to rape Miranda; and, on meeting Stephano and Trinculo, he reveres Stephano as a god and urges him not only to kill Prospero but also to take Miranda to bed so that she will 'bring . . . forth brave brood'.

The case *for* Caliban is equally obvious. He complains to Prospero: 'This island's mine, . . . / Which thou tak'st from me.' Legalistic commentators may claim that Caliban, being illegitimate, cannot lawfully claim to own property; but Caliban was *de facto* owner (if anyone could be) and is now obliged to be Prospero's slave, his power usurped by the usurped Duke. Prospero, with aristocratic obtuseness, takes it for granted that the menial tasks must be undertaken by someone other than himself or his daughter. Perhaps he, and not Caliban, is the 'toad' in this 'imaginary garden'. Though sometimes surly and vengeful, Caliban can resemble an overgrown child, over-awed by the unfamiliar. If he is unduly impressed on meeting Stephano and Trinculo, his response is not wholly unlike that of Miranda when she famously declares, on beholding Alonso's group, 'O brave new world, / That has such people in't!'; and of the same group he says: 'O Setebos, these be brave spirits indeed!' Caliban is responsive to the beauties and harmonies to which others are blind and deaf.

Whereas Stephano and Trinculo, having prosaic imaginations, appropriately talk in prose, Caliban's utterances are predominantly in verse. When his two drunken companions become preoccupied with trivia (the garments that they find), it is Caliban who rebukes them. Eventually, having been punished, reasonably leniently, by Prospero and having learned from experience, Caliban says:

> I'll be wise hereafter,
> And seek for grace. What a thrice-double ass
> Was I, to take this drunkard for a god,
> And worship this dull fool!

In seeking for grace, he seems to be wiser than Sebastian and Antonio, who remain suspiciously silent on the topic of penitence. Perhaps Caliban's quest may be completed on the island, in rueful reflections; alternatively, perhaps he may seek human guidance, sailing with Prospero and the others to the mainland.

Critical and theatrical interpretations run the risk of simplifying the complexity of Caliban. A politically right-wing interpretation will be tempted to idealise Prospero as the resourceful ruler of the island who successfully struggles to control a dangerous, anarchic and brutal force. A politically left-wing interpretation will be tempted to treat Prospero as the harsh coloniser and Caliban as the exploited victim of colonialism. The Romantic Movement looked sympathetically on rebels and the downtrodden, and in 1818 William Hazlitt, the radical literary critic, argued that Caliban was the legitimate ruler of the island and that Prospero and Miranda were the usurpers.[8] Paul MacDonnell, in 1840, declared Caliban a resister of 'tyranny'.[9] By the late twentieth century, critics and directors commonly interpreted the play as an allegory of colonialism, though there was some significant resistance to this view. In 1993, Brian Vickers argued thus in *Appropriating Shakespeare*:

> Prospero's stay on the island . . . is enforced, not voluntary, and while he can use its natural resources to stay alive, all the normal features of the hated colonist – murdering the natives, stealing their land, exporting their goods, produce, and wealth for profit back to one's home country – are conspicuously lacking. If modern critics want to denounce colonialism they should do so by all means, but this is the wrong play.[10]

Perhaps Vickers' view, in turn, may seem insufficiently flexible when we recall the complexities of *The Tempest*. It is a drama which inevitably, in many modern observers, evokes ideas of colonialist domination and of prejudice directed against those subordinated by colonialism. To make such evocation the dominant feature of the play is, however, reductive: indeed, to interpret *The Tempest* as primarily political may itself be regarded as a form of colonisation, for the interpreter is seeking to subordinate the play's multiplicity to his or her own values and prejudices. This comedy is no political tract but a work of entertainment, and it offers a voluntary and hypothetical experience of co-ordinated diversity. It combines strange escapism with earthy realities, farcical clowning with a lyrically philosophical fantasia, and an elegantly concluded plot with a disturbing open-endedness. (What *will* happen subsequently on the mainland? Will the ageing Prospero, no longer possessed of magic, again be threatened by Antonio?)

The appeal of *The Tempest* lies largely in its quality of multi-faceted richness and transformational complexity. Productions for stage and screen have repeatedly unfolded new possibilities. Peter Hall and Peter Brook are among the directors who, in reaction against more lyrical and romantic interpretations, have emphasised the dark, harsh, and even anarchic potentialities of the work. Memorable film versions include those by Derek Jarman and Peter Greenaway, while a science-fiction adaptation, *Forbidden Planet*, has generated the stage musical, *Return to the Forbidden Planet*. The influence of *The Tempest* has extended to poems and novels: examples include Shelley's 'Ariel to Miranda', Browning's 'Caliban upon Setebos', Auden's *The Sea and the Mirror*, Wells's *The Island of Dr. Moreau*, Conrad's *Victory* and Fowles's *The Magus*. All this suggests that one secret of Shakespeare's durability is his combination of amplitude, ambiguity and reticence. He offers, with abundant eloquence, a diversity of possibilities; but the ambiguity and reticence generate gaps, puzzles and enigmas, so that other people are drawn into collaboration with him. As *The Tempest* moves through time, it becomes a multiplying body of challenges and opportunities. It is a perennially transformable play of transformations.

NOTES TO THE INTRODUCTION

1 Marianne Moore: 'Poetry': in her *Collected Poems* (London: Faber and Faber, 1951), p. 41.

2 William Congreve, in the Preface to his *Incognita* (1692), said that romances deal with noble people, 'miraculous Contingencies and impossible Performances', whereas novels are 'of a more familiar nature' and offer more plausible events. See *Incognita*, ed. H. F. B. Brett-Smith (Oxford: Blackwell, 1922), pp. 5–6.

3 In the Prologue to *Every Man in His Humour*, Jonson mocks plays in which, as in Shakespeare's romances, a character proceeds from youth to age, a Chorus 'wafts you o'er the seas', a rolled bullet mimics thunder, and a drum rumbles 'to tell you when the storm doth come'. (In the Induction to *Bartholomew Fair*, Jonson says he will not offer such unnatural devices as a 'servant-monster', i.e. Caliban.).

4 Lodovico Castelvetro: *Poetica d'Aristotele vulgarizzata e sposta* [1570] (Rome: Laterza, 1978), Vol. 1, pp. 240–41. He said:

> [I]t is evident that, in tragedy and comedy, the plot contains one action only, or two that by their interdependence can be considered one . . . , because the space of time, of twelve hours at most, in which the action is represented, and the strait limits of the place in which it is represented likewise, do not permit a multitude of actions.

(This translation is in F. E. Halliday's *A Shakespeare Companion 1564–1964*; Harmondsworth: Penguin, 1964; p. 37.) Sir Philip Sidney's *Apologie for Poetrie* (written around 1580, published in 1595) insisted that 'the stage should always represent but one place, and the uttermost time presupposed in it should be . . . but one day'.

5 *Classical Literary Criticism*, translated by T. S. Dorsch (Harmondsworth: Penguin, 1965), p. 38.

6 Prospero abandons his 'art', his 'rough magic', to return to his dukedom on the mainland of Italy. Shakespeare, around this time, retired from his career as a theatrical artist and returned to his large house in Stratford-upon-Avon. Numerous commentators have regarded *The Tempest* as Shakespeare's valedictory play. (The epilogue of *A Midsummer Night's Dream* solicits applause but lacks the valedictory resonance of Prospero's epilogue.)

7 Charles G. Leland: *The English Gipsies and Their Language* (London: Kegan Paul, Trench, Trübner, 1893), p. 84.

8 Hazlitt remarks:

> Caliban . . . is strictly the legitimate sovereign of the isle, and Prospero and the rest are usurpers, who have ousted him from his hereditary jurisdiction by superiority of talent and knowledge.

(This quotation is from *The Romantics on Shakespeare*, ed. Jonathan Bate; London: Penguin, 1992; pp. 536-7.)

9 MacDonnell is cited in A. T. Vaughan and V. M. Vaughan: *Shakespeare's Caliban* (Cambridge: Cambridge University Press, 1991), p. 105.

10 Brian Vickers: *Appropriating Shakespeare* (New Haven and London: Yale University Press, 1993), p. 246.

FURTHER READING
(in chronological order)

G. Wilson Knight: *The Shakespearian Tempest*. London: Oxford University Press, 1932; London: Methuen, 1953; reprinted, 1960.

Derek Traversi: *Shakespeare: The Last Phase*. London: Hollis & Carter, 1954; rpt., 1973.

Anne Righter: *Shakespeare and the Idea of the Play*. London: Chatto & Windus, 1962; Harmondsworth: Penguin, 1967.

A. D. Nuttall: *Two Concepts of Allegory*. London: Routledge & Kegan Paul, 1967.

Shakespeare: 'The Tempest': A Casebook, ed. D. J. Palmer. London: Macmillan, 1968; revised edition: Basingstoke and London: Macmillan, 1991.

John Russell Brown: *Shakespeare: 'The Tempest'*. London: Arnold, 1969.

Twentieth-Century Interpretations of 'The Tempest': A Collection of Critical Essays, ed. Hallett Smith. Englewood Cliffs, N.J.: Prentice-Hall, 1969.

Shakespearian Comedy (Stratford-upon-Avon Studies, 14), ed. Malcolm Bradbury and David Palmer. London: Arnold, 1972.

Leslie A. Fiedler: *The Stranger in Shakespeare*. London: Croom Helm, 1973.

Narrative and Dramatic Sources of Shakespeare, Vol. VIII, ed. Geoffrey Bullough. London: Routledge & Kegan Paul; New York: Columbia University Press; 1975.

Samuel Schoenbaum: *William Shakespeare: A Compact Documentary Life*. London and New York: Oxford University Press, 1977; rpt., 1987.

Ralph Berry: *The Shakespearian Metaphor: Studies in Language and Form*. London and Basingstoke: Macmillan, 1978.

The Woman's Part: Feminist Criticism of Shakespeare, ed. Carolyn Ruth Swift Lenz *et al.* Urbana and Chicago: University of Illinois Press, 1980.

Terry Eagleton: *William Shakespeare*. Oxford: Blackwell, 1986.

Modern Critical Interpretations: William Shakespeare's 'The Tempest', ed. Harold Bloom. New York and Philadelphia: Chelsea House, 1988.

Shakespeare Survey, Vol. 43, ed. Stanley Wells. Cambridge: Cambridge University Press, 1991.

Alden T. Vaughan and Virginia Mason Vaughan: *Shakespeare's Caliban: A Cultural History*. Cambridge: Cambridge University Press, 1991.

Major Literary Characters: Caliban, ed. Harold Bloom. New York and Philadelphia: Chelsea House, 1992.

Brian Vickers: *Appropriating Shakespeare: Contemporary Critical Quarrels*. New Haven and London: Yale University Press, 1993.

Russ McDonald: *The Bedford Companion to Shakespeare*. New York: St Martin's Press; Basingstoke: Macmillan; 1996.

Post-Colonial Shakespeares, ed. Ania Loomba and Martin Orkin. London and New York: Routledge, 1998.

Kenneth S. Rothwell: *A History of Shakespeare on Screen: A Century of Film and Television*. Cambridge: Cambridge University Press, 1999.

John Sutherland and Cedric Watts: *Henry V, War Criminal? and Other Shakespeare Puzzles*. Oxford: Oxford University Press, 2000.

The Cambridge Companion to Shakespeare, ed. Margreta de Grazia and Stanley Wells. Cambridge: Cambridge University Press, 2001.

Websites:

World Shakespeare Bibliography Online: http://www-english. tamu.edu/wsb/

All Shakespeare: http://www.allshakespeare.com/

Shakespeare Online: http://www.shakespeare-online.com/

NOTE ON SHAKESPEARE

Details of Shakespeare's early life are scanty. He was the son of a prosperous merchant of Stratford-upon-Avon, and tradition gives his date of birth as 23 April, 1564; certainly, three days later, he was christened at the parish church. It is likely that he attended the local Grammar School but had no university education. Of his early career there is no record, though John Aubrey reports a claim that he was a country schoolmaster. In 1582 Shakespeare married Anne Hathaway, with whom he had two daughters, Susanna and Judith, and a son, Hamnet, who died in 1596. How he became involved with the stage in London is uncertain, but he was sufficiently established as a playwright by 1592 to be criticised in print as a challengingly versatile 'upstart Crow'. He was a leading member of the Lord Chamberlain's company, which became the King's Men on the accession of James I in 1603. Being not only a playwright and actor but also a 'sharer' and 'householder' (one of the owners of the company, entitled to a share of the profits), Shakespeare prospered greatly, as is proven by the numerous records of his financial transactions. Towards the end of his life, he loosened his ties with London and retired to New Place, the large house in Stratford which he had bought in 1597. He died on 23 April, 1616, and is buried in the place of his baptism, Holy Trinity Church. The earliest collected edition of his plays, the First Folio, was published in 1623, and its prefatory verse-tributes include Ben Jonson's famous declaration, 'He was not of an age, but for all time'.

ACKNOWLEDGEMENTS AND TEXTUAL MATTERS

I have consulted, and am indebted to, numerous editions of *The Tempest*, particularly those by: Horace Howard Furness (1892; reprinted, New York: Dover, 1964); Sir Arthur Quiller-Couch and John Dover Wilson (London: Cambridge University Press, 1921; reprinted, 1957); Frank Kermode (London: Methuen, 1954; reprinted, 1964); G. Blakemore Evans *et al.* (*The Riverside Shakespeare*: Boston, Mass.: Houghton Mifflin, 1974); Stephen Orgel (Oxford: Oxford University Press, 1987; reprinted, 1994); and Stephen Greenblatt *et al.* (*The Norton Shakespeare*: New York and London: Norton, 1997). I am also grateful for the friendly help of Prof. Mario Curreli and Dr. Hugh Drake.

The earliest extant text of *The Tempest* is that published in the First Folio (F1), the first collected edition of Shakespeare's plays, prepared by two leading members of his company, John Heminge and Henry Condell. This was published in 1623, seven years after the playwright's death. As no early Quarto texts of *The Tempest* are known, the editorial task is more straightforward than in the case of such plays as *Hamlet* or *King Lear*, which have diverse early forms. In the First Folio, the text of *The Tempest* is of good quality. It has few evident corruptions, and the stage-directions are often unusually full. The punctuation is, by the standards of those times, reasonably careful. According to various scholars, a likely explanation of the good quality of the Folio *Tempest* is that it was prepared by Ralph Crane, a 'scrivener' or professional scribe, who copied a manuscript by Shakespeare or a fair copy of one. Occasionally, however, verse is set as prose, and vice versa; and a passage now at 1.2.301-5 solicits emendation, as I explain in its endnote. Another problem is presented by Ariel's song, 'Come unto these yellow sands': F1 leaves obscure the extent of the refrain sung by spirits, and editors differ considerably in their distribution of the words. My version is closer to F1 than are most current editions.

In this Wordsworth text of *The Tempest*, I have, as is customary, modernised various spellings, some of the punctuation and some stage-directions (while occasionally adding new directions). In certain cases, I have chosen to preserve archaic spellings which seem aurally preferable. One example is that, unlike most editors, I have kept 'Millaine' instead of changing it to 'Milan'. The reason is that 'Millaine' (which, unlike 'Milan' to modern ears, is accented on the first syllable) preserves the metre and strengthens some patterns of euphony. Such archaisms are explained in the Glossary. The F1 text abounds in colons, and I have retained plenty of them. I have also retained more parentheses (brackets) than is customary, because parenthetical phrasing sometimes solicits a tone different from – and more appropriate than – that of equivalent phrasing marked off merely by commas.

The end-notes of this volume draw attention to particular textual problems and options. You will also find there examples of differences between the modernised text and the F1 version.

THE TEMPEST

CHARACTERS IN THE PLAY

PROSPERO, *rightful Duke of Millaine (Milan).*

MIRANDA, *Prospero's daughter.*

ARIEL, *a spirit serving Prospero.*

Other serving SPIRITS *appearing as 'shapes', hounds, etc., and as characters (deities, nymphs and shepherds) in a masque.*

CALIBAN, *Prospero's slave.*

ALONSO, *King of Naples.*

SEBASTIAN, *Alonso's brother.*

FERDINAND, *Alonso's son.*

ANTONIO, *Prospero's brother, the usurping Duke of Millaine.*

GONZALO, *an elderly councillor.*

STEPHANO, *Alonso's butler.*

TRINCULO, *Alonso's jester.*

MASTER *of a ship.*

BOATSWAIN.

MARINERS.

ADRIAN *and* FRANCISCO, *Lords.*

THE TEMPEST

ACT I, SCENE I.

Main deck of ship. A tempestuous noise of thunder and lightning heard.[1]

Enter SHIP-MASTER *and* BOATSWAIN.

MASTER   Boatswain!

BOATSWAIN   Here, master: what cheer?

MASTER   Good; speak to th' mariners: fall to't – yarely – or we
run ourselves aground. Bestir, bestir.   [*Exit.*

Enter MARINERS.[2]

BOATSWAIN   Heigh my hearts! Cheerly, cheerly my hearts! Yare,
yare: take in the topsail; tend to th' master's whistle.
[*To the gale:*] Blow till thou burst thy wind, if room
enough!

Enter ALONSO, SEBASTIAN, ANTONIO, FERDINAND,
GONZALO *and* OTHERS.

ALONSO   Good boatswain, have care. Where's the master? [*To
the mariners:*] Play the men.   10

BOATSWAIN   I pray now, keep below.

ANTONIO   Where is the master, bosun?[3]

BOATSWAIN   Do you not hear him? You mar our labour. Keep your
cabins: you do assist the storm.

GONZALO   Nay, good, be patient.

BOATSWAIN   When the sea is. Hence! What cares these roarers for
the name of king?[4] To cabin; silence! Trouble us not.

GONZALO   Good, yet remember whom thou hast aboard.

BOATSWAIN   None that I more love than myself. You are a councillor: if you can command these elements to silence,   20
and work the peace of the present, we will not hand a
rope more: use your authority. If you cannot, give
thanks you have lived so long, and make yourself ready
in your cabin for the mischance of the hour, if it so hap.
– Cheerly, good hearts! – Out of our way, I say.

[*Exit.*

GONZALO   I have great comfort from this fellow. Methinks he
hath no drowning mark upon him: his complexion is

perfect gallows.⁵ Stand fast, good Fate, to his hanging;
make the rope of his destiny our cable, for our own
doth little advantage. If he be not born to be hanged, 30
our case is miserable.   [*Exeunt.*

Enter BOATSWAIN.

BOATSWAIN Down with the topmast: yare, lower, lower! Bring her
to try with main-course. ⁶ [*A cry is heard within.*] A
plague upon this howling! They are louder than the
weather or our office.

Enter SEBASTIAN, ANTONIO *and* GONZALO.

Yet again? What do you here? Shall we give o'er and
drown? Have you a mind to sink?

SEBASTIAN A pox o' your throat, you bawling, blasphemous, in-
charitable dog!

BOATSWAIN Work you, then.   40

ANTONIO Hang, cur; hang, you whoreson, insolent noise-maker!
We are less afraid to be drowned than thou art.

GONZALO I'll warrant him for drowning, though the ship were
no stronger than a nutshell, and as leaky as an unstaunched wench.

BOATSWAIN Lay her a-hold, a-hold! Set her two courses: off to sea
again! Lay her off!⁷

Enter MARINERS, *wet.*

MARINERS All lost! To prayers, to prayers! All lost!

BOATSWAIN What, must our mouths be cold?

GONZALO The King and Prince at prayers, let's assist them,   50
For our case is as theirs.

SEBASTIAN   I'm out of patience.

ANTONIO We are merely cheated of our lives by drunkards.
This wide-chapped rascal – would thou mightst
                                         lie drowning
The washing of ten tides!⁸

GONZALO   He'll be hanged yet,
Though every drop of water swear against it,
And gape at wid'st to glut him.

VOICES WITHIN⁹   Mercy on us! –
We split, we split! – Farewell, my wife and children! –
Farewell, brother! – We split, we split, we split!

ANTONIO   Let's all sink wi' th' King.

SEBASTIAN   Let's take leave of him.

                          [*Exeunt Antonio and Sebastian.*

GONZALO   Now would I give a thousand furlongs of sea for an 60
           acre of barren ground: long heath, brown furze,[10] any-
           thing. The wills above be done, but I would fain die a
           dry death!   [*Exeunt.*

SCENE 2.

An island. Before Prospero's cell.

Enter PROSPERO *(wearing a cloak and bearing a staff) with* MIRANDA.[11]

MIRANDA   If by your art,[12] my dearest father, you have
           Put the wild waters in this roar, allay them.
           The sky, it seems, would pour down stinking pitch,
           But that the sea, mounting to th' welkin's cheek,
           Dashes the fire out. O! I have suffered
           With those that I saw suffer: a brave vessel
           (Who had no doubt some noble creature in her)
           Dashed all to pieces: O, the cry did knock
           Against my very heart! Poor souls, they perished.
           Had I been any god of power, I would   10
           Have sunk the sea within the earth, or ere
           It should the good ship so have swallowed and
           The fraughting souls within her.

PROSPERO   Be collected;
           No more amazement: tell your piteous heart
           There's no harm done.

MIRANDA   O woe the day!

PROSPERO   No harm:
           I have done nothing but in care of thee
           (Of thee, my dear one; thee, my daughter), who
           Art ignorant of what thou art, naught knowing
           Of whence I am, nor that I am more better
           Than Prospero, master of a full poor cell,   20
           And thy no greater father.

MIRANDA   More to know

Did never meddle with my thoughts.

PROSPERO   'Tis time
I should inform thee farther. Lend thy hand
And pluck my magic garment from me. – So,
Lie there, my art. – Wipe thou thine eyes, have
                                                            comfort.
The direful spectacle of the wrack, which touched
The very virtue of compassion in thee,
I have with such provision in mine art
So safely ordered, that there is no soul – [13]
No, not so much perdition as an hair   30
Betid to any creature in the vessel
Which thou heard'st cry, which thou saw'st sink.
                                                            Sit down,
For thou must now know farther.   [*They sit.*

MIRANDA   You have often
Begun to tell me what I am, but stopped,
And left me to a bootless inquisition,
Concluding, 'Stay: not yet.'

PROSPERO   The hour's now come;
The very minute bids thee ope thine ear.
Obey, and be attentive. Canst thou remember
A time before we came unto this cell?
I do not think thou canst, for then thou wast not   40
Out three years old.

MIRANDA   Certainly sir, I can.

PROSPERO   By what? By any other house, or person?
Of any thing the image, tell me, that
Hath kept with thy remembrance.

MIRANDA   'Tis far off,
And rather like a dream, than an assurance
That my remembrance warrants. Had I not
Four or five women once, that tended me?

PROSPERO   Thou hadst; and more, Miranda. But how is it,
That this lives in thy mind? What seest thou else
In the dark backward and abysm of time?   50
If thou rememb'rest aught ere thou cam'st here,
How thou cam'st here thou mayst.

MIRANDA   But that I do not.

PROSPERO   Twelve year since, Miranda, twelve year since,
Thy father was the Duke of Millaine[14] and
A prince of power.

MIRANDA   Sir, are not you my father?

PROSPERO   Thy mother was a piece of virtue, and
She said thou wast my daughter; and thy father
Was Duke of Millaine, and his only heir
A princess, no worse issued.[15]

MIRANDA   O the heavens!
What foul play had we, that we came from thence?   60
Or blessèd was't we did?

PROSPERO   Both, both, my girl.
By foul play, as thou sayst, were we heaved thence,
But blessedly holp hither.

MIRANDA   O, my heart bleeds
To think o'th' teen that I have turned you to,
Which is from my remembrance. Please you,
                           farther.

PROSPERO   My brother, and thy uncle, called Antonio –
I pray thee mark me, that a brother should
Be so perfidious – he, whom next thyself
Of all the world I loved, and to him put
The manage of my state, as at that time   70
Through all the signories it was the first,
And Prospero the prime duke, being so reputed
In dignity, and for the liberal arts[16]
Without a parallel; those being all my study,
The government I cast upon my brother,
And to my state grew stranger, being transported
And rapt in secret studies. Thy false uncle –
Dost thou attend me?

MIRANDA   Sir, most heedfully.

PROSPERO   – Being once pérfected how to grant suits,
How to deny them, who t'advance, and who   80
To trash for over-topping, new created
The creatures that were mine, I say, or changed 'em,
Or else new formed 'em; having both the key
Of officer and office, set all hearts i'th' state

	To what tune pleased his ear, that now he was
	The ivy which had hid my princely trunk,
	And sucked my verdure out on't – Thou attend'st not!
MIRANDA	O good sir, I do.
PROSPERO	I pray thee mark me. –

	I, thus neglecting worldly ends, all dedicated	
	To closeness and the bettering of my mind	90
	With that which, but by being so retired,	
	O'er-prized all popular rate,[17] in my false brother	
	Awaked an evil nature; and my trust,	
	Like a good parent,[18] did beget of him	
	A falsehood in its contrary, as great	
	As my trust was, which had indeed no limit,	
	A confidence sans bound. He, being thus lorded	
	Not only with what my revénue yielded	
	But what my power might else exact, like one	
	Who having unto truth, by telling of it,	100
	Made such a sinner of his memory	
	To credit his own lie,[19] he did believe	
	He was indeed the Duke, out o'th' substitution	
	And executing th'outward face of royalty	
	With all prerogative.[20] Hence his ambition growing –	
	Dost thou hear?	
MIRANDA	Your tale, sir, would cure deafness.	
PROSPERO	– To have no screen between this part he played	
	And him he played it for, he needs will be	
	Absolute Millaine. Me, poor man, my library	
	Was dukedom large enough: of temporal royalties	110
	He thinks me now incapable; confederates	
	(So dry he was for sway) wi'th' King of Naples	
	To give him annual tribute, do him homage,	
	Subject his coronet to his crown, and bend	
	The dukedom yet unbowed (alas, poor Millaine!)	
	To most ignoble stooping.	
MIRANDA	O the heavens!	
PROSPERO	Mark his condition, and th'event; then tell me	
	If this might be a brother.	
MIRANDA	I should sin	
	To think but nobly of my grandmother:[21]	

Good wombs have borne bad sons.

PROSPERO   Now the condition: 120
This King of Naples, being an enemy
To me inveterate, hearkens my brother's suit,
Which was that he, in lieu o'th' premises
Of homage, and I know not how much tribute,
Should presently extírpate me and mine
Out of the dukedom, and confer fair Millaine,
With all the honours, on my brother. Whereon,
A treacherous army levied, one midnight,
Fated to th' purpose, did Antonio open
The gates of Millaine, and i'th' dead of darkness   130
The ministers for th' purpose hurried thence
Me and thy crying self.

MIRANDA   Alack, for pity:
I not remembring how I cried out then
Will cry it o'er again: it is a hint
That wrings mine eyes to't.

PROSPERO   Hear a little further,
And then I'll bring thee to the present business
Which now's upon's: without the which, this story
Were most impertinent.

MIRANDA   Wherefore did they not
That hour destroy us?

PROSPERO   Well demanded, wench:
My tale provokes that question. Dear, they durst not,   140
So dear the love my people bore me; nor set
A mark so bloody on the business; but
With colours fairer painted their foul ends.
In few, they hurried us aboard a bark,
Bore us some leagues to sea; where they prepared
A rotten carcass of a butt, not rigged,
Nor tackle, sail, nor mast: the very rats
Instinctively have quit it. There they hoist us
To cry to th' sea, that roared to us; to sigh
To th' winds, whose pity, sighing back again,   150
Did us but loving wrong.

MIRANDA   Alack, what trouble

Was I then to you!

PROSPERO   O, a cherubin
Thou wast that did preserve me. Thou didst smile,
Infusèd with a fortitude from heaven,
When I have decked the sea with drops full salt,
Under my burthen groaned; which raised in me
An undergoing stomach, to bear up
Against what should ensue.

MIRANDA   How came we ashore?

PROSPERO By Providence divine.[22]
Some food we had, and some fresh water, that   160
A noble Neapolitan, Gonzalo,
Out of his charity, who being then appointed
Master of this design, did give us, with
Rich garments, linens, stuffs, and necessaries
Which since have steaded much. So of his gentleness,
Knowing I loved my books, he furnished me
From mine own library with volumes that
I prize above my dukedom.

MIRANDA   Would I might
But ever see that man!

PROSPERO [rising:]   Now I arise;
Sit still, and hear the last of our sea-sorrow.   170
                              [He dons his mantle.
Here in this island we arrived, and here
Have I, thy schoolmaster, made thee more profit
Than other princess' can,[23] that have more time
For vainer hours, and tutors not so careful.

MIRANDA Heaven thank you for't. And now, I pray you sir,
For still 'tis beating in my mind, your reason
For raising this sea-storm?

PROSPERO   Know thus far forth.
By accident most strange, bountiful Fortune
(Now my dear lady) hath mine enemies
Brought to this shore; and by my prescience   180
I find my zenith doth depend upon
A most auspicious star, whose influence
If now I court not, but omit, my fortunes

Will ever after droop. Here cease more questions:
Thou art inclined to sleep; 'tis a good dulness,
And give it way: I know thou canst not choose.

> [*Miranda sleeps.*

– Come away, servant, come! I am ready now.
Approach, my Ariel.[24] Come!

Enter ARIEL.

ARIEL
All hail, great master; grave sir, hail! I come
To answer thy best pleasure: be't to fly,   190
To swim, to dive into the fire, to ride
On the curled clouds, to thy strong bidding task
Ariel and all his quality.

PROSPERO
                         Hast thou, spirit,
Performed to point the tempest that I bade thee?

ARIEL
To every article.
I boarded the King's ship: now on the beak,
Now in the waist, the deck, in every cabin,
I flamed amazement. Sometimes I'd divide
And burn in many places: on the topmast,
The yards and boresprit would I flame distinctly,   200
Then meet and join. Jove's lightning, the precursors
O'th' dreadful thunder-claps, more momentary
And sight-outrunning were not; the fire and cracks
Of sulphurous roaring the most mighty Neptune
Seem to besiege, and make his bold waves tremble,
Yea, his dread trident shake.[25]

PROSPERO
                              My brave spirit!
Who was so firm, so constant, that this coil
Would not infect his reason?

ARIEL
                            Not a soul
But felt a fever of the mad, and played
Some tricks of desperation; all but mariners   210
Plunged in the foaming brine, and quit the vessel,
Then all afire with me: the King's son Ferdinand,[26]
With hair up-staring (then like reeds, not hair),
Was the first man that leapt; cried 'Hell is empty,
And all the devils are here!'

PROSPERO
                            Why, that's my spirit!

But was not this nigh shore?

ARIEL   Close by, my master.

PROSPERO   But are they, Ariel, safe?

ARIEL   Not a hair perished:
On their sustaining garments not a blemish,
But fresher than before; and, as thou bad'st me,
In troops I have dispersed them 'bout the isle.   220
The King's son have I landed by himself,
Whom I left cooling of the air with sighs,
In an odd angle of the isle, and sitting,
His arms in this sad knot.

PROSPERO   Of the King's ship,
The mariners, say how thou hast disposed,
And all the rest o'th' fleet.

ARIEL   Safely in harbour
Is the King's ship: in the deep nook, where once
Thou called'st me up at midnight to fetch dew
From the still-vexed Bermoothès, there she's hid;
The mariners all under hatches stowed,   230
Who, with a charm joined to their suffered labour,
I have left asleep; and for the rest o'th' fleet,
Which I dispersed, they all have met again,
And are upon the Mediterranean flote
Bound sadly home for Naples,
Supposing that they saw the King's ship wracked,
And his great person perish.

PROSPERO   Ariel, thy charge
Exactly is performed; but there's more work.
What is the time o'th' day?

ARIEL   Past the mid-season.

PROSPERO   At least two glasses. The time 'twixt six and now   240
Must by us both be spent most preciously.[27]

ARIEL   Is there more toil? Since thou dost give me pains,
Let me remember thee what thou hast promised,
Which is not yet performed me.

PROSPERO   How now? Moody?
What is't thou canst demand?

ARIEL   My liberty.

PROSPERO Before the time be out? No more!

ARIEL   I prithee,
Remember I have done thee worthy service,
Told thee no lies, made no mistakings, served
Without or grudge or grumblings; thou didst promise
To bate me a full year.

PROSPERO   Dost thou forget   250
From what a torment I did free thee?

ARIEL   No.

PROSPERO Thou dost, and think'st it much to tread the ooze
Of the salt deep,
To run upon the sharp wind of the north,
To do me business in the veins o'th'earth
When it is baked with frost.

ARIEL   I do not, sir.

PROSPERO Thou liest, malignant thing! Hast thou forgot
The foul witch Sycorax, who with age and envy
Was grown into a hoop?[28] Hast thou forgot her?

ARIEL No, sir.

PROSPERO   Thou hast. Where was she born? Speak: tell me. 260

ARIEL Sir, in Argier.

PROSPERO   O, was she so? I must
Once in a month recount what thou hast been,
Which thou forget'st. This damned witch Sycorax,
For mischiefs manifold, and sorceries terrible
To enter human hearing, from Argier
Thou know'st was banished; for one thing she did
They would not take her life.[29] Is not this true?

ARIEL Ay, sir.

PROSPERO This blue-eyed hag was hither brought with child,
And here was left by th' sailors. Thou, my slave,   270
As thou report'st thyself, was then her servant,
And for thou wast a spirit too delicate
To act her earthy and abhorred commands,
Refusing her grand hests, she did confine thee,
By help of her more potent ministers,
And in her most unmitigable rage,
Into a cloven pine: within which rift
Imprisoned, thou didst painfully remain

	A dozen years: within which space she died,
	And left thee there: where thou didst vent thy groans 280
	As fast as mill-wheels strike. Then was this island
	(Save for the son that she did litter here,
	A freckled whelp, hag-born) not honoured with
	A human shape.
ARIEL	Yes: Caliban her son.
PROSPERO	Dull thing, I say so: he, that Caliban
	Whom now I keep in service. Thou best know'st
	What torment I did find thee in: thy groans
	Did make wolves howl, and penetrate the breasts
	Of ever-angry bears; it was a torment
	To lay upon the damned, which Sycorax 290
	Could not again undo. It was mine art,
	When I arrived and heard thee, that made gape
	The pine, and let thee out.
ARIEL	I thank thee, master.
PROSPERO	If thou more murmur'st, I will rend an oak
	And peg thee in his knotty entrails till
	Thou hast howled away twelve winters.
ARIEL	Pardon, master.
	I will be correspondent to command,
	And do my spriting gently.
PROSPERO	Do so: and after two days
	I will discharge thee.
ARIEL	That's my noble master!
	What shall I do? Say what: what shall I do? 300
PROSPERO	Go make thyself like a nymph o'th' sea; be subject
	To no sight but thine and mine, invisible
	To every eye-ball else: go take this shape,
	And hither come in't. Go: hence,
	With diligence.[30] [*Exit Ariel.*
	– Awake, dear heart, awake, thou hast slept well;
	Awake.
MIRANDA	The strangeness of your story put
	Heaviness in me.
PROSPERO	Shake it off. Come on;
	We'll visit Caliban, my slave, who never

Yields us kind answer.

MIRANDA   'Tis a villain, sir,   310
I do not love to look on.

PROSPERO   But, as 'tis,
We cannot miss him: he does make our fire,
Fetch in our wood, and serves in offices
That profit us. – What ho! Slave! Caliban!
Thou earth, thou! Speak.

CALIBAN [*within:*]   There's wood enough within.

PROSPERO Come forth, I say; there's other business for thee.
Come, thou tortoise, when?

     Enter ARIEL *like a water-nymph.*

Fine apparition! My quaint Ariel,
Hark in thine ear. [*He whispers.*]

ARIEL   My lord, it shall be done.   [*Exit.*

PROSPERO [*to Caliban:*] Thou poisonous slave, got by the devil
                       himself   320
Upon thy wicked dam:[31] come forth.

     Enter CALIBAN.

CALIBAN As wicked dew as e'er my mother brushed
With raven's feather from unwholesome fen
Drop on you both! A south-west blow on ye,
And blister you all o'er!

PROSPERO For this, be sure, tonight thou shalt have cramps,
Side-stitches that shall pen thy breath up; urchins
Shall, for that vast of night that they may work,
All exercise on thee:[32] thou shalt be pinched
As thick as honeycomb, each pinch more stinging   330
Than bees had made 'em.

CALIBAN   I must eat my dinner.
This island's mine, by Sycorax my mother,[33]
Which thou tak'st from me. When thou cam'st first,
Thou strok'st me, and made much of me; wouldst
                       give me
Water with berries in't, and teach me how
To name the bigger light, and how the less,
That burn by day and night:[34] and then I loved thee,
And showed thee all the qualities o'th'isle,

The fresh springs, brine-pits, barren place and fertile.
Curst be I that did so! All the charms   340
Of Sycorax, toads, beetles, bats, light on you:
For I am all the subjects that you have,
Which first was mine own king; and here you sty me
In this hard rock, whiles you do keep from me
The rest o'th'island.

PROSPERO   Thou most lying slave,
Whom stripes may move, not kindness! I have
                                    used thee
(Filth as thou art) with húmane care, and lodged thee
In mine own cell, till thou didst seek to violate
The honour of my child.

CALIBAN   O ho, O ho! Would't had been done!   350
Thou didst prevent me; I had peopled else
This isle with Calibans.

MIRANDA   Abhorrèd slave,
Which any print of goodness will not take,
Being capable of all ill! I pitied thee,
Took pains to make thee speak, taught thee each hour
One thing or other: when thou didst not, savage,
Know thine own meaning, but wouldst gabble like
A thing most brutish, I endowed thy purposes
With words that made them known. But thy vile race,
Though thou didst learn, had that in't which
                                    good natures   360
Could not abide to be with; therefore wast thou
Deservedly confined into this rock,
Who hadst deserved more than a prison.

CALIBAN   You taught me language, and my profit on't
Is, I know how to curse: the red plague rid you,
For learning me your language.

PROSPERO   Hag-seed, hence!
Fetch us in fuel, and be quick – thou'rt best –
To answer other business.[35] Shrug'st thou, Malice?
If thou neglect'st or dost unwillingly
What I command, I'll rack thee with old cramps,   370
Fill all thy bones with achès, make thee roar,

That beasts shall tremble at thy din.

CALIBAN   No, pray thee.
[*Aside:*] I must obey; his art is of such power,
It would control my dam's god Setebos,
And make a vassal of him.

PROSPERO   So, slave, hence!
                                        [*Exit Caliban.*

Enter ARIEL, *invisible to others, playing and singing,*
FERDINAND *following. Prospero and Miranda stand aside.*

ARIEL [*sings:*]   Come unto these yellow sands,
                     And then take hands;
                     Curtsied when you have and kissed
                     (The wild waves whist),[36]
                     Foot it featly here and there,   380
                     And, sweet sprites, bear
                     The burthen.[37]

SPIRITS [*dispersedly within:*]
                     Hark, hark!
                          'Bow-wow!'
                     The watch dogs bark:
                          'Bow-wow!'

ARIEL   Hark, hark:
                          I hear
                     The strain of strutting Chanticleer
                          Cry 'Cockadiddle-dow!'   390

FERDINAND Where should this music be? I'th'air, or th'earth?
          It sounds no more; and sure it waits upon
          Some god o'th'island. Sitting on a bank,
          Weeping again the King my father's wrack,
          This music crept by me upon the waters,
          Allaying both their fury and my passion
          With its sweet air: thence I have followed it
          (Or it hath drawn me rather); but 'tis gone.
          No, it begins again.

ARIEL [*sings:*]   Full fathom five thy father lies.
                          Of his bones are coral made;
                     Those are pearls that were his eyes;   400
                          Nothing of him that doth fade,

But doth suffer a sea-change
Into something rich and strange.
Sea-nymphs hourly ring his knell.

SPIRITS [*within:*]   Ding-dong.

ARIEL [*sings:*]   Hark: now I hear them: ding-dong bell.

FERDINAND The ditty does remember my drowned father.
[*Music.*] This is no mortal business, nor no sound   410
That the earth owes: I hear it now above me.

PROSPERO [*to Miranda:*] The fringèd curtains of thine eye
advance,
And say what thou seest yond.[38]

MIRANDA   What is't? A spirit?
Lord, how it looks about. Believe me, sir,
It carries a brave form. But 'tis a spirit.

PROSPERO No, wench; it eats and sleeps, and hath such senses
As we have, such. This gallant which thou seest
Was in the wrack; and but he's something stained
With grief (that's beauty's canker), thou mightst
call him
A goodly person. He hath lost his fellows,   420
And strays about to find 'em.

MIRANDA   I might call him
A thing divine, for nothing natural
I ever saw so noble.

PROSPERO [*aside:*]   It goes on, I see,
As my soul prompts it. [*To Ariel:*] Spirit, fine spirit,
I'll free thee
Within two days for this.

FERDINAND [*seeing Miranda:*]   Most sure, the goddess
On whom these airs attend! – Vouchsafe my prayer
May know if you remain upon this island,[39]
And that you will some good instruction give
How I may bear me here. My prime request,
Which I do last pronounce, is – O you wonder![40] –   430
If you be maid, or no?

MIRANDA   No wonder, sir,
But certainly a maid.

FERDINAND   My language? Heavens!

I am the best of them that speak this speech,
Were I but where 'tis spoken.[41]

PROSPERO   How? The best?
What wert thou if the King of Naples heard thee?

FERDINAND A single thing, as I am now, that wonders
To hear thee speak of Naples. He does hear me,
And that he does, I weep: myself am Naples,
Who with mine eyes, never since at ebb, beheld
The King my father wracked.

MIRANDA   Alack, for mercy!   440

FERDINAND Yes, faith, and all his lords, the Duke of Millaine
And his brave son being twain.[42]

PROSPERO [aside:]   The Duke of
                                   Millaine
And his more braver daughter could control thee,
If now 'twere fit to do't. At the first sight
They have changed eyes. – Delicate Ariel,
I'll set thee free for this. [To Ferdinand:] A word,
                                 good sir.
I fear you have done yourself some wrong; a word.

MIRANDA Why speaks my father so ungently? This
Is the third man that ever I saw; the first
That e'er I sighed for. Pity move my father   450
To be inclined my way.

FERDINAND   O, if a virgin,
And your affection not gone forth, I'll make you
The Queen of Naples.

PROSPERO   Soft, sir: one word more.
[Aside:] They are both in either's powers; but this swift
                                   business
I must uneasy make, lest too light winning
Make the prize light. [To Ferdinand:] One word more:
                                 I charge thee
That thou attend me. Thou dost here usurp
The name thou ow'st not, and hast put thyself
Upon this island as a spy, to win it
From me, the lord on't.

FERDINAND   No, as I am a man.   460

MIRANDA There's nothing ill can dwell in such a temple.

If the ill spirit have so fair a house,
Good things will strive to dwell with't.

PROSPERO [*to Ferdinand:*]   Follow me.
[*To Miranda:*] Speak not you for him: he's a traitor.
                              [*To Ferdinand:*] Come:
I'll manacle thy neck and feet together;
Sea-water shalt thou drink; thy food shall be
The fresh-brook mussels, withered roots, and husks
Wherein the acorn cradled. Follow.

FERDINAND   No:
I will resist such entertainment till
Mine enemy has more power.
[*He draws his sword, but is paralysed by Prospero's magic.*[43]

MIRANDA   O dear father,   470
Make not too rash a trial of him, for
He's gentle, and not fearful.

PROSPERO   What, I say,
My foot my tutor?[44] – Put thy sword up, traitor,
Who mak'st a show, but dar'st not strike, thy
                                        conscience
Is so possessed with guilt. Come from thy ward,
For I can here disarm thee with this stick,
And make thy weapon drop.
                    [*Ferdinand's sword falls from his hand.*

MIRANDA   Beseech you, father.

PROSPERO Hence! Hang not on my garments.

MIRANDA   Sir, have pity;
I'll be his surety.

PROSPERO   Silence. One word more
Shall make me chide thee, if not hate thee. What,   480
An advocate for an impostor? Hush!
Thou think'st there is no more such shapes as he,
Having seen but him and Caliban. Foolish wench,
To th' most of men, this is a Caliban,
And they to him are angels.

MIRANDA   My affections
Are then most humble: I have no ambition
To see a goodlier man.

PROSPERO [*to Ferdinand:*]   Come on, obey:

Thy nerves are in their infancy again,
And have no vigour in them.

FERDINAND   So they are:
My spirits, as in a dream, are all bound up.   490
My father's loss, the weakness which I feel,
The wrack of all my friends, nor this man's threats,[45]
To whom I am subdued, are but light to me,
Might I but through my prison once a day
Behold this maid. All corners else o'th'earth
Let liberty make use of; space enough
Have I in such a prison.

PROSPERO   [aside:]   It works.
                    [To Ferdinand:] Come on.
            [To Ariel:] Thou hast done well, fine Ariel.
                             [To Ferdinand:] Follow me.
            [To Ariel:] Hark what thou else shalt do me.

MIRANDA   [to Ferdinand:]   Be of comfort;
My father's of a better nature, sir,   500
Than he appears by speech: this is unwonted
Which now came from him.

PROSPERO   [to Ariel:]   Thou shalt be as free
As mountain winds; but then exactly do
All points of my command.

ARIEL   To th' syllable.

PROSPERO   [to Ferdinand:] Come, follow.
                    [To Miranda:] Speak not for him.
                                        [Exeunt.

ACT 2, SCENE 1.

Another part of the island.

Enter ALONSO, SEBASTIAN, ANTONIO, GONZALO,
ADRIAN *and* FRANCISCO.

GONZALO   [*to Alonso:*] Beseech you, sir, be merry; you have cause,
So have we all, of joy; for our escape
Is much beyond our loss. Our hint of woe
Is common; every day some sailor's wife,
The masters of some merchant, and the merchant,
Have just our theme of woe. But for the miracle –
I mean our preservation – few in millions
Can speak like us: then wisely, good sir, weigh
Our sorrow with our comfort.

ALONSO   Prithee, peace.

SEBASTIAN   [*to Antonio:*] He receives comfort like cold porridge.[46] 10

ANTONIO   The visitor will not give him o'er so.

SEBASTIAN   Look, he's winding up the watch of his wit; by and by
it will strike.

GONZALO   [*to Alonso:*] Sir –

SEBASTIAN   [*to Antonio:*] One: tell.

GONZALO   When every grief is entertained that's offered,
Comes to the entertainer –

SEBASTIAN   [*aloud:*] A dollar.

GONZALO   Dolour comes to him indeed: you have spoken truer
than you purposed.[47]   20

SEBASTIAN   You have taken it wiselier than I meant you should.

GONZALO   [*to Alonso:*] Therefore, my lord, –

ANTONIO   [*to Sebastian:*] Fie, what a spendthrift is he of his tongue.

ALONSO   [*to Gonzalo:*] I prithee, spare.

GONZALO   Well, I have done; but yet –

SEBASTIAN   [*to Antonio:*] He will be talking.

ANTONIO   Which, of he or Adrian, – for a good wager – first
begins to crow?

SEBASTIAN   The old cock.

ANTONIO   The cockerel.   30

SEBASTIAN	Done. The wager?
ANTONIO	A laughter.[48]
SEBASTIAN	A match!
ADRIAN	[*to Gonzalo:*] Though this island seem to be desert, –
ANTONIO	Ha, ha, ha!
SEBASTIAN	So, you're paid.
ADRIAN	Uninhabitable, and almost inaccessible, –
SEBASTIAN	Yet –
ADRIAN	Yet –
ANTONIO	He could not miss't.

40

ADRIAN   It must needs be of subtle, tender and delicate temperance.

ANTONIO   'Temperance' was a delicate wench.

SEBASTIAN Ay, and a subtle, as he most learnedly delivered.

ADRIAN   The air breathes upon us here most sweetly.

SEBASTIAN As if it had lungs, and rotten ones.

ANTONIO   Or, as 'twere perfumed by a fen.

GONZALO   Here is every thing advantageous to life.

ANTONIO   True, save means to live.

SEBASTIAN Of that there's none, or little.

50

GONZALO   How lush and lusty the grass looks! How green!

ANTONIO   The ground, indeed, is tawny.

SEBASTIAN With an eye of green in't.

ANTONIO   He misses not much.

SEBASTIAN No: he doth but mistake the truth totally.

GONZALO   But the rarity of it is, which is indeed almost beyond credit, –

SEBASTIAN As many vouched rarities are.

GONZALO   That our garments, being, as they were, drenched in the sea, hold notwithstanding their freshness and glosses, 60 being rather new-dyed than stained with salt water.

ANTONIO   If but one of his pockets could speak, would it not say he lies?

SEBASTIAN Ay, or very falsely pocket up his report.

GONZALO   Methinks our garments are now as fresh as when we put them on first in Afric, at the marriage of the King's fair daughter Claribel to the King of Tunis.

SEBASTIAN 'Twas a sweet marriage, and we prosper well in our return.

ADRIAN	Tunis was never graced before with such a paragon to 70 their queen.
GONZALO	Not since widow Dido's time.
ANTONIO	[to Sebastian:] 'Widow'? A pox o'that! How came that 'widow' in? 'Widow Dido'!
SEBASTIAN	What if he had said 'widower Aeneas' too? Good Lord, how you take it!
ADRIAN	[to Gonzalo:] Widow Dido, said you? You make me study of that: she was of Carthage, not of Tunis.⁴⁹
GONZALO	This Tunis, sir, was Carthage.
ADRIAN	Carthage? 80
GONZALO	I assure you, Carthage.
ANTONIO	[to Sebastian:] His word is more than the miraculous harp.
SEBASTIAN	He hath raised the wall, and houses too.⁵⁰
ANTONIO	What impossible matter will he make easy next?
SEBASTIAN	I think he will carry this island home in his pocket, and give it his son for an apple.
ANTONIO	And, sowing the kernels of it in the sea, bring forth more islands.
GONZALO	[to Adrian:] Ay. 90
ANTONIO	[to Sebastian:] Why, in good time.
GONZALO	[to Alonso:] Sir, we were talking, that our garments seem now as fresh as when we were at Tunis at the marriage of your daughter, who is now queen.
ANTONIO	And the rarest that e'er came there.
SEBASTIAN	Bate, I beseech you, widow Dido.
ANTONIO	O, widow Dido! Ay, widow Dido.
GONZALO	[to Alonso:] Is not, sir, my doublet as fresh as the first day I wore it – I mean, in a sort –
ANTONIO	[to Sebastian:] That sort was well fished for.⁵¹ 100
GONZALO	When I wore it at your daughter's marriage?
ALONSO	You cram these words into mine ears, against The stomach of my sense.⁵² Would I had never Married my daughter there: for, coming thence, My son is lost; and, in my rate, she too, Who is so far from Italy removed, I ne'er again shall see her. O thou mine heir Of Naples and of Millaine, what strange fish

    Hath made his meal on thee?

FRANCISCO   Sir, he may live.
I saw him beat the surges under him,   110
And ride upon their backs; he trod the water,
Whose enmity he flung aside, and breasted
The surge most swoll'n that met him; his bold head
'Bove the contentious waves he kept, and oared
Himself with his good arms in lusty stroke
To th' shore, that o'er his wave-worn basis bowed,
As stooping to relieve him. I not doubt
He came alive to land.

ALONSO   No, no; he's gone.

SEBASTIAN Sir, you may thank yourself for this great loss,
That would not bless our Europe with your daughter, 120
But rather lose her to an African,
Where she, at least, is banished from your eye,
Who hath cause to wet the grief on't.

ALONSO   Prithee, peace.

SEBASTIAN You were kneeled to and impórtuned otherwise
By all of us: and the fair soul herself
Weighed between loathness and obedience, at
Which end o'th' beam should bow.[53] We have
                                 lost your son,
I fear, for ever. Millaine and Naples have
Mo widows in them of this business' making
Than we bring men to comfort them: 130
The fault's your own.

ALONSO   So is the dear'st o'th' loss.

GONZALO My lord Sebastian,
The truth you speak doth lack some gentleness,
And time to speak it in: you rub the sore,
When you should bring the plaster.

SEBASTIAN   Very well.

ANTONIO And most chirurgeonly.

GONZALO [to Alonso:] It is foul weather in us all, good sir,
When you are cloudy.

SEBASTIAN   Fowl weather?[54]

ANTONIO   Very foul.

GONZALO [to Alonso:] Had I plantation of this isle, my lord, –

ANTONIO	He'd sow't with nettle-seed.
SEBASTIAN	Or docks, or mallows. 140
GONZALO	And were the king on't, what would I do?
SEBASTIAN	Scape being drunk, for want of wine.
GONZALO	I'th' commonwealth I would by contraries
	Execute all things: for no kind of traffic
	Would I admit; no name of magistrate;
	Letters should not be known; riches, poverty,
	And use of service, none; contract, succession,
	Bourn, bound of land, tilth, vineyard, none;
	No use of metal, corn, or wine, or oil;
	No occupation, all men idle, all, 150
	And women too, but innocent and pure;
	No sovereignty –
SEBASTIAN	Yet he would be king on't.
ANTONIO	The latter end of his commonwealth forgets the
	beginning.
GONZALO	All things in common nature should produce
	Without sweat or endeavour. Treason, felony,
	Sword, pike, knife, gun, or need of any engine,
	Would I not have; but nature should bring forth,
	Of it own kind, all foison, all abundance,
	To feed my innocent people.[55]
SEBASTIAN	[to Antonio:] No marrying 'mong his subjects? 160
ANTONIO	None, man, all idle: whores and knaves.
GONZALO	[to Alonso:] I would with such perfection govern, sir,
	T'excel the Golden Age.[56]
SEBASTIAN	God save his Majesty![57]
ANTONIO	Long live Gonzalo!
GONZALO	And – do you mark me, sir?
ALONSO	Prithee, no more: thou dost talk nothing to me.
GONZALO	I do well believe your Highness, and did it to minister occasion to these gentlemen, who are of such sensible and nimble lungs, that they always use to laugh at nothing.
ANTONIO	'Twas you we laughed at. 170
GONZALO	Who, in this kind of merry fooling, am nothing to you: so you may continue, and laugh at nothing still.
ANTONIO	What a blow was there given!

SEBASTIAN An it had not fallen flat-long.

GONZALO You are gentlemen of brave mettle: you would lift the
moon out of her sphere, if she would continue in it
five weeks without changing.[58]

Enter ARIEL, *invisible to them, playing solemn music.*

SEBASTIAN We would so, and then go a-batfowling.[59]

ANTONIO [*to Gonzalo:*] Nay, good my lord, be not angry.

GONZALO No, I warrant you. I will not adventure my discretion   180
so weakly. Will you laugh me asleep? For I am very
heavy.

ANTONIO Go sleep, and hear us.

                              [*Gonzalo, Adrian and Francisco sleep.*

ALONSO What, all so soon asleep? I wish mine eyes
Would, with themselves, shut up my thoughts. I find
They are inclined to do so.

SEBASTIAN   Please you, sir,
Do not omit the heavy offer of it:
It seldom visits sorrow; when it doth,
It is a comforter.

ANTONIO   We two, my lord,
Will guard your person while you take your rest,   190
And watch your safety.

ALONSO   Thank you. Wondrous heavy.

                        [*Alonso sleeps. Exit Ariel.*

SEBASTIAN What a strange drowsiness possesses them!

ANTONIO It is the quality o'th' climate.

SEBASTIAN   Why
Doth it not then our eyelids sink? I find not
Myself disposed to sleep.

ANTONIO   Nor I; my spirits are nimble.
They fell together all, as by consent;
They dropped, as by a thunder-stroke. What might,
Worthy Sebastian, O what might – ? No more.
And yet, methinks, I see it in thy face,
What thou shouldst be: th'occasion speaks thee,[60] and   200
My strong imagination sees a crown
Dropping upon thy head.

SEBASTIAN   What? Art thou waking?

ANTONIO   Do you not hear me speak?

SEBASTIAN   I do, and surely
           It is a sleepy language, and thou speak'st
           Out of thy sleep. What is it thou didst say?
           This is a strange repose, to be asleep
           With eyes wide open; standing, speaking, moving,
           And yet so fast asleep.

ANTONIO   Noble Sebastian,
           Thou let'st thy fortune sleep – die rather; wink'st
           Whiles thou art waking.

SEBASTIAN   Thou dost snore distinctly;   210
           There's meaning in thy snores.

ANTONIO   I am more serious than my custom. You
           Must be so too, if heed me: which to do,
           Trebles thee o'er.

SEBASTIAN   Well: I am standing water.

ANTONIO   I'll teach you how to flow.

SEBASTIAN   Do so; to ebb,
           Hereditary sloth instructs me.⁶¹

ANTONIO   O,
           If you but knew how you the purpose cherish
           Whiles thus you mock it; how, in stripping it,
           You more invest it! Ebbing men, indeed,
           Most often, do so near the bottom run   220
           By their own fear, or sloth.

SEBASTIAN   Prithee, say on.
           The setting of thine eye and cheek proclaim
           A matter from thee, and a birth, indeed,
           Which throes thee much to yield.

ANTONIO   Thus, sir:
           Although this lord of weak remembrance, this,
           Who shall be of as little memory
           When he is earthed, hath here almost persuaded
           (For he's a spirit of persuasion, only
           Professes to persuade)⁶² the King his son's alive,
           'Tis as impossible that he's undrowned,   230
           As he that sleeps here swims.

SEBASTIAN   I have no hope

           That he's undrowned.

ANTONIO   O, out of that 'no hope',
What great hope have you! No hope, that way, is
Another way so high an hope, that even
Ambition cannot pierce a wink beyond,
But doubt discovery there.[63] Will you grant with me
That Ferdinand is drowned?

SEBASTIAN   He's gone.

ANTONIO   Then, tell me,
Who's the next heir of Naples?

SEBASTIAN   Claribel.

ANTONIO   She that is Queen of Tunis: she that dwells
Ten leagues beyond man's life:[64] she that from Naples   240
Can have no note (unless the sun were post:
The man i'th' moon's too slow) till new-born chins
Be rough and razorable; she that from whom[65]
We all were sea-swallowed, though some cast again
(And that by destiny) to perform an act,
Whereof what's past is prologue; what to come,
In yours and my discharge.

SEBASTIAN What stuff is this? How say you?
'Tis true, my brother's daughter's Queen of Tunis;
So is she heir of Naples; 'twixt which regions   250
There is some space.

ANTONIO   A space whose every cubit
Seems to cry out, 'How shall that Claribel
Measure us back to Naples? Keep in Tunis,
And let Sebastian wake.' Say this were death
That now hath seized them – why, they were no
                                   worse
Than now they are. There be that can rule Naples
As well as he that sleeps; lords, that can prate
As amply and unnecessarily
As this Gonzalo: I myself could make
A chough of as deep chat.[66] O, that you bore   260
The mind that I do; what a sleep were this
For your advancement! Do you understand me?

SEBASTIAN Methinks I do.

ANTONIO   And how does your content

Tender your own good fortune?

SEBASTIAN   I remember
You did supplant your brother Prospero.

ANTONIO   True;
And look how well my garments sit upon me,
Much feater than before. My brother's servants
Were then my fellows; now they are my men.

SEBASTIAN But, for your conscience?

ANTONIO Ay, sir: where lies that? If 'twere a kibe,   270
'Twould put me to my slipper; but I feel not
This deity in my bosom. Twenty consciences,
That stand 'twixt me and Millaine, candied be they,
And melt ere they molest![67] Here lies your brother,
No better than the earth he lies upon,
If he were that which now he's like – that's dead;
Whom I with this obedient steel, three inches of it,
Can lay to bed for ever; whiles you, doing thus,
To the perpetual wink for aye might put
This ancient morsel, this Sir Prudence, who   280
Should not upbraid our course. For all the rest,
They'll take suggestion as a cat laps milk;
They'll tell the clock to any business that
We say befits the hour.

SEBASTIAN   Thy case, dear friend,
Shall be my precedent: as thou got'st Millaine,
I'll come by Naples. Draw thy sword. One stroke
Shall free thee from the tribute which thou payest,
And I the King shall love thee.

ANTONIO   Draw together;
And when I rear my hand, do you the like
To fall it on Gonzalo.   [*They draw their swords.*

SEBASTIAN   O, but one word.   290
                              [*They talk apart.*

          Music. Enter ARIEL, *unseen by them.*

ARIEL   [*to Gonzalo:*] My master, through his art, foresees
                                        the danger
That you, his friend, are in, and sends me forth
(For else his project dies) to keep them living.

[*He sings in Gonzalo's ear:*]
    While you here do snoring lie,
    Open-eyed conspiracy
      His time doth take.
    If of life you keep a care,
    Shake off slumber, and beware.
      Awake! Awake!

ANTONIO [*to Sebastian:*] Then let us both be sudden.

GONZALO [*waking:*]   Now, good angels 300
    Preserve the King!   [*The others wake.*

ALONSO Why, how now? Ho! Awake! Why are you drawn?
    Wherefore this ghastly looking?

GONZALO   What's the matter?

SEBASTIAN Whiles we stood here securing your repose,
    Even now, we heard a hollow burst of bellowing,
    Like bulls, or rather lions: did't not wake you?
    It struck mine ear most terribly.

ALONSO   I heard nothing.

ANTONIO O, 'twas a din to fright a monster's ear –
    To make an earthquake! Sure, it was the roar
    Of a whole herd of lions.

ALONSO   Heard you this, Gonzalo? 310

GONZALO Upon mine honour, sir, I heard a humming –
    And that a strange one too – which did awake me.
    I shaked you, sir, and cried. As mine eyes opened,
    I saw their weapons drawn. There was a noise,
    That's verily. 'Tis best we stand upon our guard,
    Or that we quit this place. Let's draw our weapons.

ALONSO Lead off this ground, and let's make further search
    For my poor son.

GONZALO   Heavens keep him from these beasts;
    For he is, sure, i'th'island.

ALONSO   Lead away.
         [*Exeunt all but Ariel.*

ARIEL Prospero, my lord, shall know what I have done. 320
    So, King, go safely on to seek thy son.
            [*Exit.*

SCENE 2.

Another part of the island.

Enter CALIBAN, *with a burden of wood. Thunder heard.*

CALIBAN   All the infections that the sun sucks up
From bogs, fens, flats, on Prosper fall, and make him
By inch-meal a disease! [*Thunder.*] His spirits hear me,
And yet I needs must curse. But they'll nor pinch,
Fright me with urchin-shows, pitch me i'th' mire,
Nor lead me, like a firebrand in the dark,
Out of my way, unless he bid 'em; but
For every trifle are they set upon me:
Sometime like apes, that mow and chatter at me,
And after bite me; then like hedgehogs, which   10
Lie tumbling in my barefoot way, and mount
Their pricks at my footfall; sometime am I
All wound with adders, who with cloven tongues
Do hiss me into madness –

Enter TRINCULO.

                Lo, now, lo!
Here comes a spirit of his, and to torment me
For bringing wood in slowly. I'll fall flat.
Perchance he will not mind me.   [*He lies concealed*
                              beneath his gaberdine.

TRINCULO Here's neither bush nor shrub to bear off any weather
at all, and another storm brewing. I hear it sing i'th'
wind. Yond same black cloud, yond huge one, looks 20
like a foul bombard that would shed his liquor. If it
should thunder, as it did before, I know not where to
hide my head: yond same cloud cannot choose but fall
by pailfuls. [*He sees Caliban.*] What have we here? A
man or a fish? Dead or alive? A fish, he smells like a
fish; a very ancient and fish-like smell; a kind of not-
of-the-newest poor-John: a strange fish. Were I in
England now (as once I was), and had but this fish
painted, not a holiday fool there but would give a piece

of silver: there would this monster make a man. Any 30
strange beast there makes a man: when they will not give
a doit to relieve a lame beggar, they will lay out ten to
see a dead Indian. Legged like a man; and his fins like
arms. Warm, o' my troth! I do now let loose my
opinion, hold it no longer: this is no fish, but an islander,
that hath lately suffered by a thunderbolt. [*Thunder.*]
Alas, the storm is come again. My best way is to creep
under his gaberdine: there is no other shelter hereabout.
Misery acquaints a man with strange bed-fellows. I will
here shroud till the dregs of the storm be past. 40

He hides. Enter STEPHANO, *singing; a wooden bottle in his hand.*

STEPHANO   I shall no more to sea, to sea;
     Here shall I die ashore, −
This is a very scurvy tune to sing at a man's funeral:
Well, here's my comfort.   [*He drinks.*
[*He sings:*]
   The master, the swabber, the boatswain, and I,
    The gunner, and his mate,
   Loved Mall, Meg, and Marian, and Margery,
    But none of us cared for Kate;
     For she had a tongue with a tang,
     Would cry to a sailor, 'Go hang!' 50
   She loved not the savour of tar nor of pitch,
   Yet a tailor might scratch her where'er she did itch.[68]
    Then to sea, boys, and let her go hang!
This is a scurvy tune too: but here's my comfort.
            [*He drinks.*

CALIBAN   [*to Trinculo:*] Do not torment me! O!
STEPHANO What's the matter? Have we devils here? Do you put
tricks upon's with salvages and men of Inde, ha? I have
not scaped drowning to be afeard now of your four legs:
for it hath been said: 'As proper a man as ever went on
four legs[69] cannot make him give ground'; and it shall be 60
said so again, while Stephano breathes at nostrils.
CALIBAN   The spirit torments me! O!
STEPHANO This is some monster of the isle, with four legs; who
hath got, as I take it, an ague. Where the devil should
he learn our language? I will give him some relief, if it

be but for that. If I can recover him, and keep him
tame, and get to Naples with him, he's a present for
any emperor that ever trod on neat's-leather.

CALIBAN   Do not torment me, prithee! I'll bring my wood home
faster.   70

STEPHANO   He's in his fit now, and does not talk after the wisest.
He shall taste of my bottle: if he have never drunk
wine afore, it will go near to remove his fit. If I can
recover him, and keep him tame, I will not take too
much for him;[70] he shall pay for him that hath him, and
that soundly.

CALIBAN   Thou dost me yet but little hurt; thou wilt anon, I know
it by thy trembling. Now Prosper works upon thee.

STEPHANO   Come on your ways: open your mouth: here is that
which will give language to you, cat.[71] Open your   80
mouth; this will shake your shaking, I can tell you, and
that soundly. [*Caliban drinks, but flinches.*] You cannot
tell who's your friend; open your chaps again.

TRINCULO   I should know that voice. It should be – but he is
drowned; and these are devils; O, defend me!

STEPHANO   Four legs and two voices: a most delicate monster. His
forward voice now is to speak well of his friend; his
backward voice is to utter foul speeches, and to de-
tract. If all the wine in my bottle will recover him, I
will help his ague. Come. [*Caliban drinks again.*] Amen.   90
I will pour some in thy other mouth.

TRINCULO   Stephano!

STEPHANO   Doth thy other mouth call me? Mercy, mercy! This is
a devil, and no monster: I will leave him – I have no
long spoon.[72]

TRINCULO   Stephano! If thou beest Stephano, touch me, and speak
to me: for I am Trinculo – be not afeard – thy good
friend Trinculo.

STEPHANO   If thou beest Trinculo, come forth. I'll pull thee by the
lesser legs. If any be Trinculo's legs, these are they.   100
[*Trinculo emerges.*] Thou art very Trinculo, indeed!
How cam'st thou to be the siege of this moon-calf?
Can he vent Trinculos?

TRINCULO   [*rising:*] I took him to be killed with a thunder-stroke. But

art thou not drowned, Stephano? I hope now, thou art
not drowned. Is the storm overblown? I hid me under the
dead moon-calf's gaberdine, for fear of the storm. And art
thou living, Stephano? O Stephano, two Neapolitans
scaped!

STEPHANO Prithee do not turn me about, my stomach is not 110
constant.

CALIBAN [aside:] These be fine things, and if they be not sprites!
That's a brave god, and bears celestial liquor:
I will kneel to him.   [Caliban kneels.

STEPHANO [to Trinculo:] How didst thou scape? How cam'st thou
hither? Swear by this bottle, how thou cam'st hither. I
escaped upon a butt of sack which the sailors heaved
o'er-board – by this bottle, which I made of the bark of
a tree with mine own hands since I was cast ashore.

CALIBAN I'll swear upon that bottle to be thy true subject, for 120
the liquor is not earthly.

STEPHANO [to Trinculo:] Here; swear then how thou escaped'st.

TRINCULO Swam ashore, man, like a duck. I can swim like a duck,
I'll be sworn.

STEPHANO Here, kiss the book.[73] [Trinculo drinks.] Though thou
canst swim like a duck, thou art made like a goose.

TRINCULO O Stephano, hast any more of this?

STEPHANO The whole butt, man. My cellar is in a rock by th' sea-
side, where my wine is hid. [To Caliban:] How now,
moon-calf? How does thine ague?   130

CALIBAN Hast thou not dropped from heaven?

STEPHANO Out o'th' moon, I do assure thee. I was the man i'th'
moon, when time was.

CALIBAN I have seen thee in her, and I do adore thee. My
mistress showed me thee, and thy dog and thy bush.[74]

STEPHANO Come, swear to that: kiss the book. I will furnish it
anon with new contents. Swear. [Rising, Caliban drinks.

TRINCULO By this good light, this is a very shallow monster! I afeard
of him? A very weak monster. 'The man i'th' moon'! A
most poor credulous monster. [Caliban empties bottle.] 140
Well drawn, monster, in good sooth.

CALIBAN I'll show thee every fertile inch of the island;
And I will kiss thy foot. I prithee be my god.

TRINCULO   By this light, a most perfidious and drunken monster.
           When's god's asleep, he'll rob his bottle.

CALIBAN   [to Stephano:] I'll kiss thy foot. I'll swear myself thy subject.

STEPHANO   Come on then: down, and swear.   [Caliban kneels.

TRINCULO   I shall laugh myself to death at this puppy-headed
           monster: a most scurvy monster: I could find in my
           heart to beat him —   150

STEPHANO   Come, kiss.   [Caliban kisses his foot.

TRINCULO   But that the poor monster's in drink. An abominable
           monster!

CALIBAN   I'll show thee the best springs; I'll pluck thee berries;
           I'll fish for thee, and get thee wood enough.
           A plague upon the tyrant that I serve!
           I'll bear him no more sticks, but follow thee,
           Thou wondrous man.

TRINCULO   A most ridiculous monster, to make a wonder of a
           poor drunkard!   160

CALIBAN   I prithee, let me bring thee where crabs grow;
           And I with my long nails will dig thee pig-nuts;
           Show thee a jay's nest, and instruct thee how
           To snare the nimble marmoset: I'll bring thee
           To clustring filberts, and sometimes I'll get thee
           Young scamels[75] from the rock. Wilt thou go with me?

STEPHANO   I prithee now, lead the way without any more talking. —
           Trinculo, the King and all our company else being
           drowned, we will inherit here. [To Caliban:] Here; bear
           my bottle. — Fellow Trinculo, we'll fill him by and by   170
           again.

CALIBAN   [sings drunkenly:] Farewell master; farewell, farewell.

TRINCULO   A howling monster; a drunken monster.

CALIBAN   [sings:] No more dams I'll make for fish,
                      Nor fetch in firing
                        At requiring,
                   Nor scrape trenchering, nor wash dish.
                      'Ban, 'Ban, Ca-Caliban
                      Has a new master. Get a new man!
           Freedom, high-day! High-day, freedom! Freedom,   180
           high-day, freedom!

STEPHANO   O brave monster; lead the way.   [Exeunt.

ACT 3, SCENE 1.

Before Prospero's cell.

Enter FERDINAND, *bearing a log.*

FERDINAND There be some sports are painful, and their labour
Delight in them sets off;[76] some kinds of baseness
Are nobly undergone; and most poor matters
Point to rich ends. This my mean task
Would be as heavy to me as odious, but
The mistress which I serve quickens what's dead,
And makes my labours pleasures. O, she is
Ten times more gentle than her father's crabbed;
And he's composed of harshness. I must remove
Some thousands of these logs, and pile them up,   10
Upon a sore injunction. My sweet mistress
Weeps when she sees me work, and says such baseness
Had never like executor.[77] I forget;
But these sweet thoughts do even refresh my labours –
Most busil'est when I do it.[78]

Enter MIRANDA, *followed by* PROSPERO *at a distance.*

MIRANDA   Alas, now pray you,
Work not so hard. I would the lightning had
Burnt up those logs that you are enjoined to pile.
Pray set it down, and rest you. When this burns,
'Twill weep for having wearied you. My father
Is hard at study; pray now, rest yourself;   20
He's safe for these three hours.

FERDINAND   O most dear mistress,
The sun will set before I shall discharge
What I must strive to do.

MIRANDA   If you'll sit down,
I'll bear your logs the while: pray give me that;
I'll carry it to the pile.

FERDINAND   No, precious creature,
I had rather crack my sinews, break my back,
Than you should such dishonour undergo

                    While I sit lazy by.
MIRANDA   It would become me
                    As well as it does you; and I should do it
                    With much more ease: for my good will is to it,   30
                    And yours it is against.
PROSPERO   [aside:]   Poor worm, thou art infected,
                    This visitation shown it.
MIRANDA   You look wearily.
FERDINAND   No, noble mistress, 'tis fresh morning with me
                    When you are by at night. I do beseech you,
                    Chiefly that I might set it in my prayers,
                    What is your name?
MIRANDA   Miranda. – O my father,
                    I have broke your hest to say so!
FERDINAND   Admired Miranda!
                    Indeed the top of admiration, worth
                    What's dearest to the world! Full many a lady
                    I have eyed with best regard, and many a time   40
                    Th' harmony of their tongues hath into bondage
                    Brought my too diligent ear. For several virtues
                    Have I liked several women; never any
                    With so full soul, but some defect in her
                    Did quarrel with the noblest grace she owed,
                    And put it to the foil.[79] But you, O you,
                    So perfect, and so peerless, are created
                    Of every creature's best.
MIRANDA   I do not know
                    One of my sex; no woman's face remember,
                    Save, from my glass, mine own; nor have I seen   50
                    More that I may call men than you, good friend,
                    And my dear father. How features are abroad,
                    I am skilless of; but, by my modesty
                    (The jewel in my dower), I would not wish
                    Any companion in the world but you;
                    Nor can imagination form a shape,
                    Besides yourself, to like of. But I prattle
                    Something too wildly, and my father's precepts
                    I therein do forget.
FERDINAND   I am, in my condition,

A prince, Miranda; I do think, a king –   60
I would not so! – and would no more endure
This wooden slavery, than to suffer
The flesh-fly blow my mouth. Hear my
                          soul speak:
The very instant that I saw you, did
My heart fly to your service; there resides
To make me slave to it; and for your sake
Am I this patient log-man.

MIRANDA   Do you love me?

FERDINAND O heaven, O earth, bear witness to this sound,
And crown what I profess with kind event
If I speak true; if hollowly, invert   70
What best is boded me to mischief! I,
Beyond all limit of what else i'th' world,
Do love, prize, honour you.

MIRANDA   I am a fool
To weep at what I am glad of.

PROSPERO [*aside:*]   Fair encounter
Of two most rare affections: heavens rain grace
On that which breeds between 'em!

FERDINAND   Wherefore weep you?

MIRANDA At mine unworthiness, that dare not offer
What I desire to give, and much less take
What I shall die to want. But this is trifling;
And all the more it seeks to hide itself,   80
The bigger bulk it shows. Hence, bashful cunning,
And prompt me, plain and holy innocence.
I am your wife, if you will marry me;
If not, I'll die your maid: to be your fellow
You may deny me, but I'll be your servant,
Whether you will or no.

FERDINAND [*kneeling:*]   My mistress, dearest;
And I thus humble ever.

MIRANDA   My husband then?

FERDINAND Ay, with a heart as willing
As bondage e'er of freedom: here's my hand.

MIRANDA And mine, with my heart in't; and now farewell   90

Till half an hour hence.

FERDINAND   A thousand thousand!

[*Exeunt Miranda and Ferdinand separately.*

PROSPERO So glad of this as they I cannot be,
Who are surprised with all; but my rejoicing
At nothing can be more. I'll to my book,
For yet, ere supper-time, must I perform
Much business appertaining.

[*Exit.*

SCENE 2.

Another part of the island.

Enter CALIBAN, STEPHANO *and* TRINCULO.

STEPHANO [*to Trinculo:*] Tell not me. When the butt is out we will
drink water; not a drop before. Therefore bear up, and
board 'em. [*To Caliban:*] Servant-monster, drink to me.

TRINCULO 'Servant-monster'? The folly of this island! They say
there's but five upon this isle; we are three of them. If
th'other two be brained like us, the state totters.

STEPHANO Drink, servant-monster, when I bid thee. Thy eyes are
almost set in thy head.

TRINCULO Where should they be set else? He were a brave monster
indeed, if they were set in his tail.   10

STEPHANO My man-monster hath drowned his tongue in sack; for
my part, the sea cannot drown me. I swam, ere I could
recover the shore, five-and-thirty leagues, off and on.
By this light, thou shalt be my lieutenant, monster, or
my standard.

TRINCULO Your lieutenant if you list; he's no standard.

STEPHANO We'll not run, Monsieur Monster.

TRINCULO Nor go neither; but you'll lie, like dogs, and yet say
nothing neither.

STEPHANO Moon-calf, speak once in thy life, if thou beest a good   20
moon-calf.

CALIBAN How does thy honour? Let me lick thy shoe.
I'll not serve him; he is not valiant.

TRINCULO   Thou liest, most ignorant monster; I am in case to justle a constable. Why, thou debauched fish thou, was there ever a man a coward, that hath drunk so much sack as I today? Wilt thou tell a monstrous lie, being but half a fish, and half a monster?

CALIBAN   Lo, how he mocks me! Wilt thou let him, my lord?

TRINCULO   'Lord', quoth he! That a monster should be such a 30 natural!

CALIBAN   Lo, lo, again! Bite him to death, I prithee.

STEPHANO   Trinculo, keep a good tongue in your head: if you prove a mutineer, – the next tree! The poor monster's my subject, and he shall not suffer indignity.

CALIBAN   I thank my noble lord. Wilt thou be pleased to hearken once again to the suit I made to thee?

STEPHANO   Marry will I: kneel and repeat it. I will stand, and so shall Trinculo.   [*Caliban kneels.*

Enter ARIEL, *invisible to them.*

CALIBAN   As I told thee before, I am subject to a tyrant, a 40 sorcerer, that by his cunning hath cheated me of the island.

ARIEL   Thou liest.

CALIBAN   [*to Trinculo:*] Thou liest, thou jesting monkey, thou! I would my valiant master would destroy thee. I do not lie.

STEPHANO   Trinculo, if you trouble him any more in's tale, by this hand, I will supplant some of your teeth.

TRINCULO   Why, I said nothing.

STEPHANO   Mum, then, and no more. [*To Caliban:*] Proceed.

CALIBAN   I say, by sorcery he got this isle;   50
From me he got it. If thy greatness will
Revenge it on him – for I know thou dar'st,
But this thing dare not –

STEPHANO   That's most certain.

CALIBAN   Thou shalt be lord of it, and I'll serve thee.

STEPHANO   How now shall this be compassed? Canst thou bring me to the party?

CALIBAN   Yea, yea, my lord. I'll yield him thee asleep,
Where thou mayst knock a nail into his head.[80]

ARIEL	Thou liest, thou canst not.
CALIBAN	What a pied ninny's this! – Thou scurvy patch! – 60
	I do beseech thy greatness, give him blows,
	And take his bottle from him. When that's gone,
	He shall drink nought but brine, for I'll not show him
	Where the quick freshes are.
STEPHANO	Trinculo, run into no further danger! Interrupt the
	monster one word further, and, by this hand, I'll turn
	my mercy out of doors, and make a stockfish of thee.
TRINCULO	Why, what did I? I did nothing. I'll go further off.
STEPHANO	Didst thou not say he lied?
ARIEL	Thou liest. 70
STEPHANO	Do I so? Take thou that. [*He strikes Trinculo*.] As you
	like this, give me the lie another time.
TRINCULO	I did not give the lie. Out o' your wits, and hearing
	too? A pox o' your bottle! This can sack and drinking
	do. A murrain on your monster, and the devil take
	your fingers!
CALIBAN	Ha, ha, ha!
STEPHANO	Now, forward with your tale. [*To Trinculo:*] Prithee stand
	further off.
CALIBAN	Beat him enough; after a little time, 80
	I'll beat him too.
STEPHANO	Stand further. – Come, proceed.
CALIBAN	Why, as I told thee, 'tis a custom with him
	I'th'afternoon to sleep: there thou mayst brain him,
	Having first seized his books; or with a log
	Batter his skull, or paunch him with a stake,
	Or cut his wezand with thy knife. Remember
	First to possess his books; for without them
	He's but a sot, as I am; nor hath not
	One spirit to command: they all do hate him
	As rootedly as I. Burn but his books. 90
	He has brave útensils (for so he calls them),
	Which, when he has a house, he'll deck withal.
	And that most deeply to consider is
	The beauty of his daughter. He himself
	Calls her a nonpareil: I never saw a woman
	But only Sycorax (my dam) and she;

	But she as far surpasseth Sycorax	
	As great'st does least.	
STEPHANO	Is it so brave a lass?	
CALIBAN	Ay lord, she will become thy bed, I warrant,	
	And bring thee forth brave brood.	100
STEPHANO	Monster, I will kill this man; his daughter and I will be king[81] and queen – save our graces! – and Trinculo and thyself shall be viceroys. Dost thou like the plot, Trinculo?	
TRINCULO	Excellent.	
STEPHANO	Give me thy hand. I am sorry I beat thee; but, while thou liv'st, keep a good tongue in thy head.	
CALIBAN	Within this half hour will he be asleep. Wilt thou destroy him then?	
STEPHANO	Ay, on mine honour.	
ARIEL	[*aside:*] This will I tell my master.	110
CALIBAN	Thou mak'st me merry: I am full of pleasure. Let us be jocund. Will you troll the catch You taught me but while-ere?	
STEPHANO	At thy request, monster, I will do reason, any reason. – Come on, Trinculo, let us sing.	

    STEPHANO *and* TRINCULO *sing:*

> Flout 'em, and scout 'em,
> And scout 'em, and flout 'em:
> Thought is free.

| CALIBAN | That's not the tune. | |

    ARIEL *plays the tune on a tabor and pipe.*

STEPHANO	What is this same?	120
TRINCULO	This is the tune of our catch, played by the picture of Nobody.	
STEPHANO	[*towards Ariel:*] If thou beest a man, show thyself in thy likeness; if thou beest a devil, take't as thou list.	
TRINCULO	O forgive me my sins!	
STEPHANO	He that dies, pays all debts: I defy thee. Mercy upon us!	
CALIBAN	Art thou afeard?	
STEPHANO	No, monster, not I.	
CALIBAN	Be not afeard. The isle is full of noises, Sounds and sweet airs, that give delight, and hurt not:	130

> Sometimes a thousand twangling instruments
> Will hum about mine ears; and sometime voices,
> That, if I then had waked after long sleep,
> Will make me sleep again; and then, in dreaming,
> The clouds methought would open, and show riches
> Ready to drop upon me, that when I waked,
> I cried to dream again.

STEPHANO   This will prove a brave kingdom to me, where I shall
have my music for nothing.

CALIBAN   When Prospero is destroyed.   140

STEPHANO   That shall be by and by: I remember the story.

[Exit Ariel, playing.

TRINCULO   The sound is going away. Let's follow it, and after do
our work.

STEPHANO   Lead, monster, we'll follow. I would I could see this
taborer: he lays it on.

TRINCULO   [*to Caliban:*] Wilt come? I'll follow Stephano.[82]

[Exeunt.

SCENE 3.

Another part of the island.

Enter ALONSO, SEBASTIAN, ANTONIO, GONZALO, ADRIAN *and*
FRANCISCO.

GONZALO   By'r lakin, I can go no further, sir.
My old bones ache. Here's a maze trod, indeed,
Through forthrights and meanders. By your patience,
I needs must rest me.

ALONSO   Old lord, I cannot blame thee,
Who am myself attached with weariness,
To th' dulling of my spirits. Sit down, and rest.
Even here I will put off my hope, and keep it
No longer for my flatterer. He is drowned
Whom thus we stray to find, and the sea mocks
Our frústrate search on land. Well, let him go.   10

ANTONIO   [*aside to Sebastian:*]
I am right glad that he's so out of hope.

	Do not, for one repulse, forgo the purpose
	That you resolved t'effect.
SEBASTIAN	[*aside to Antonio:*] The next advantage
	Will we take throughly.
ANTONIO	Let it be tonight,
	For, now they are oppressed with travail, they
	Will not, nor cannot, use such vigilance
	As when they are fresh.
SEBASTIAN	I say, tonight. No more.

Solemn and strange music; and PROSPER *on the top (invisible).*[83]

ALONSO	What harmony is this? My good friends, hark!
GONZALO	Marvellous sweet music!

Enter several strange SHAPES, *bringing in a banquet;*
and dance about it with gentle actions of salutations;
and, inviting the King, &c. to eat, they depart.[84]

ALONSO	Give us kind keepers, heavens! What were these? 20
SEBASTIAN	A living drollery. Now I will believe
	That there are unicorns; that in Arabia
	There is one tree, the phoenix' throne, one phoenix
	At this hour reigning there.[85]
ANTONIO	I'll believe both;
	And what does else want credit, come to me,
	And I'll be sworn 'tis true. Travellers ne'er did lie,
	Though fools at home condemn 'em.[86]
GONZALO	If in Naples
	I should report this now, would they believe me
	If I should say I saw such islanders? –
	For, certes, these are people of the island, 30
	Who, though they are of monstrous shape, yet note
	Their manners are more gentle-kind than of
	Our human generation you shall find
	Many, nay, almost any.
PROSPERO	[*aside:*] Honest lord,
	Thou hast said well: for some of you there present
	Are worse than devils.
ALONSO	I cannot too much muse;
	Such shapes, such gesture, and such sound,
	expressing

    (Although they want the use of tongue) a kind
    Of excellent dumb discourse.
PROSPERO   [*aside:*]   Praise in departing.[87]
FRANCISCO They vanished strangely.
SEBASTIAN   No matter, since   40
    They have left their viands behind; for we
              have stomachs.
    Will't please you taste of what is here?
ALONSO   Not I.
GONZALO Faith, sir, you need not fear. When we were boys,
    Who would believe that there were mountaineers
    Dewlapped like bulls, whose throats had hanging
                at 'em
    Wallets of flesh? Or that there were such men
    Whose heads stood in their breasts?[88] Which now
               we find
    Each putter-out of five for one will bring us
    Good warrant of.[89]
ALONSO   I will stand to, and feed,
    Although my last; no matter, since I feel   50
    The best is past. Brother, my lord the Duke,
    Stand to and do as we.

 Thunder and lightning. Enter ARIEL *like a harpy, claps his wings*
 upon the table, and, with a quaint device, the banquet vanishes.[90]

ARIEL   You are three men of sin, whom destiny –
    That hath to instrument this lower world
    And what is in't – the never-surfeited sea
    Hath caused to belch up you, and on this island
    Where man doth not inhabit, you 'mongst men
    Being most unfit to live. I have made you mad;
    And even with suchlike valour, men hang and drown
    Their proper selves. [*Several men draw their swords.*]
         You fools! I and my fellows   60
    Are ministers of Fate. The elements
    Of whom your swords are tempered may as well
    Wound the loud winds, or with bemocked-at stabs
    Kill the still-closing waters, as diminish
    One dowl that's in my plume; my fellow-ministers
    Are like invulnerable. If you could hurt,

Your swords are now too massy for your strengths,
And will not be uplifted. But remember
(For that's my business to you) that you three
From Millaine did supplant good Prospero;   70
Exposed unto the sea (which hath requit it)
Him and his innocent child; for which foul deed,
The powers, delaying, not forgetting, have
Incensed the seas and shores, yea, all the creatures,
Against your peace. Thee of thy son, Alonso,
They have bereft; and do pronounce by me,
Ling'ring perdition (worse than any death
Can be at once) shall step by step attend
You and your ways; whose wraths to guard
                                        you from –
Which here, in this most desolate isle, else falls   80
Upon your heads – is nothing but heart's sorrow,
And a clear life ensuing.

He vanishes in thunder. Then, to soft music, enter the SHAPES *again,
and dance with mocks and mows; and depart, carrying out the table.*[91]

PROSPERO   [*aside:*] Bravely the figure of this harpy hast thou
Performed, my Ariel; a grace it had, devouring;
Of my instruction hast thou nothing bated
In what thou hadst to say. So, with good life
And observation strange, my meaner ministers
Their several kinds have done. My high charms work,
And these, mine enemies, are all knit up
In their distractions:[92] they now are in my power;   90
And in these fits I leave them, whilst I visit
Young Ferdinand (whom they suppose is drowned)
And his and mine loved darling.   [*Exit above.*

GONZALO   I'th' name of something holy, sir, why stand you
In this strange stare?

ALONSO   O, it is monstrous, monstrous!
Methought the billows spoke, and told me of it;
The winds did sing it to me; and the thunder,
That deep and dreadful organ-pipe, pronounced
The name of Prosper: it did bass my trespass.[93]
Therefore my son i'th'ooze is bedded; and   100
I'll seek him deeper than e'er plummet sounded,

And with him there lie mudded.   [*Exit.*

SEBASTIAN   But one fiend at a time,
I'll fight their legions o'er.

ANTONIO   I'll be thy second. [*Exeunt.*

GONZALO All three of them are desperate: their great guilt,
Like poison given to work a great time after,
Now 'gins to bite the spirits. I do beseech you,
That are of suppler joints, follow them swiftly,
And hinder them from what this ecstasy
May now provoke them to.

ADRIAN [*to Francisco:*]   Follow, I pray you.
                                                  [*Exeunt.*

ACT 4, SCENE I.

Before Prospero's cell.

Enter PROSPERO, FERDINAND *and* MIRANDA.

PROSPERO [*to Ferdinand:*] If I have too austerely punished you,
Your compensation makes amends, for I
Have given you here a third of mine own life,[94]
Or that for which I live: who once again
I tender to thy hand. All thy vexations
Were but my trials of thy love, and thou
Hast strangely stood the test. Here, afore Heaven,
I ratify this my rich gift: O Ferdinand,
Do not smile at me that I boast of her,[95]
For thou shalt find she will outstrip all praise   10
And make it halt behind her.

FERDINAND   I do believe it
Against an oracle.

PROSPERO Then, as my gift,[96] and thine own acquisition
Worthily purchased, take my daughter. But
If thou dost break her virgin-knot before
All sanctimonious ceremonies may
With full and holy rite be ministered,
No sweet aspersion shall the heavens let fall
To make this contract grow; but barren hate,
Sour-eyed disdain, and discord shall bestrew   20
The union of your bed with weeds so loathly
That you shall hate it both. Therefore take heed,
As Hymen's lamp shall light you.[97]

FERDINAND   As I hope
For quiet days, fair issue, and long life,
With such love as 'tis now: the murkiest den,
The most oppórtune place, the strong'st suggestion
Our worser genius can, shall never melt
Mine honour into lust, to take away
The edge of that day's celebration,
When I shall think, or Phoebus' steeds are foundered,   30

Or Night kept chained below.[98]

PROSPERO   Fairly spoke.
Sit, then, and talk with her: she is thine own. –
What, Ariel; my industrious servant Ariel!

Enter ARIEL.

ARIEL   What would my potent master? Here I am.
PROSPERO   Thou and thy meaner fellows your last service
Did worthily perform, and I must use you
In such another trick. Go bring the rabble
(O'er whom I give thee power) here to this place.
Incite them to quick motion, for I must
Bestow upon the eyes of this young couple   40
Some vanity of mine art: it is my promise,
And they expect it from me.
ARIEL   Presently?
PROSPERO   Ay, with a twink.
ARIEL   Before you can say 'come' and 'go',
And breathe twice, and cry 'so, so',
Each one, tripping on his toe,
Will be here with mop and mow.
Do you love me, master? No?
PROSPERO   Dearly, my delicate Ariel. Do not approach
Till thou dost hear me call.
ARIEL   Well; I conceive.   [*Exit.* 50
PROSPERO   [*to Ferdinand:*]
Look thou be true. Do not give dalliance
Too much the rein: the strongest oaths are straw
To th' fire i'th' blood. Be more abstemious,
Or else good night your vow.
FERDINAND   I warrant you, sir,
The white cold virgin snow upon my heart
Abates the ardour of my liver.[99]
PROSPERO   Well. –
Now come, my Ariel. Bring a corollary,
Rather than want a spirit;[100] appear, and pertly! –
No tongue! All eyes! Be silent!   [*Soft music.*

Enter IRIS.[101]

IRIS   Ceres, most bounteous lady: thy rich leas   60
Of wheat, rye, barley, vetches, oats, and pease;
Thy turfy mountains, where live nibbling sheep,
And flat meads thatched with stover, them to keep;
Thy banks with pionèd and twillèd brims,[102]
Which spongy April at thy hest betrims
To make cold nymphs chaste crowns; and thy
                          broom-groves,
Whose shadow the dismissèd bachelor loves,
Being lass-lorn; thy pole-clipped vineyard,[103]
And thy sea-marge, sterile and rocky-hard,
Where thou thyself dost air: the Queen o'th' Sky,   70
Whose wat'ry arch and messenger am I,
Bids thee leave these, and with her sovereign grace,

A peacock-drawn chariot, bearing JUNO, *descends.*[104]

Here on this grass-plot, in this very place,
To come and sport; her peacocks fly amain.
Approach, rich Ceres, her to entertain.

Enter CERES.[105]

CERES   [*to Iris:*] Hail, many-coloured messenger, that ne'er
Dost disobey the wife of Jupiter;
Who, with thy saffron wings, upon my flowers
Diffusest honey-drops, refreshing showers,
And with each end of thy blue bow dost crown   80
My bosky acres and my unshrubbed down,
Rich scarf to my proud earth: why hath thy queen
Summoned me hither, to this short-grassed green?

IRIS   A contract of true love to celebrate,
And some donation freely to estate
On the blessed lovers.

CERES   Tell me, heavenly bow,
If Venus or her son, as thou dost know,
Do now attend the Queen. Since they did plot
The means that dusky Dis my daughter got,[106]
Her and her blind boy's scandalled company   90
I have forsworn.

IRIS   Of her society

Be not afraid. I met her deity
Cutting the clouds towards Paphos,[107] and her son
Dove-drawn with her: here thought they to have done
Some wanton charm upon this man and maid
(Whose vows are, that no bed-rite shall be paid
Till Hymen's torch be lighted); but in vain.
Mars's hot minion is returned again;
Her waspish-headed son has broke his arrows,
Swears he will shoot no more, but play with sparrows   100
And be a boy right out.[108]

                    JUNO *alights from her chariot.*

CERES   Highest Queen of state,
          Great Juno comes; I know her by her gait.
JUNO   How does my bounteous sister? Go with me
          To bless this twain, that they may prosperous be,
          And honoured in their issue.

                    JUNO *and* CERES *sing together:*[109]

          Honour, riches, marriage-blessing,
          Long continuance, and increasing,
          Hourly joys be still upon you!
          Juno sings her blessings on you.
          Earth's increase, foison plenty,   110
          Barns and garners never empty,
          Vines with clust'ring bunches growing,
          Plants with goodly burden bowing;
          Spring come to you, at the farthest,
          In the very end of harvest![110]
          Scarcity and want shall shun you;
          Ceres' blessing so is on you.

FERDINAND This is a most majestic vision, and
          Harmonious charmingly: may I be bold
          To think these spirits?
PROSPERO   Spirits, which by mine art   120
          I have from their confines called to enact
          My present fancies.
FERDINAND   Let me live here ever;
          So rare a wondered father and a wise

Makes this place Paradise.[111]

[*Juno and Ceres whisper, and send Iris on employment.*[112]

PROSPERO   Sweet now, silence:[113]
Juno and Ceres whisper seriously:
There's something else to do. Hush, and be mute,
Or else our spell is marred.

IRIS   You nymphs, called Naiads, of the windring brooks,[114]
With your sedged crowns and ever harmless looks,
Leave your crisp channels, and on this green land   130
Answer your summons; Juno does command.
Come, temperate nymphs, and help to celebrate
A contract of true love: be not too late.

                    Enter some NYMPHS.

You sunburnt sicklemen, of August weary,
Come hither from the furrow, and be merry.
Make holiday: your rye-straw hats put on,
And these fresh nymphs encounter every one
In country footing.

Enter certain REAPERS, *properly habited. They join with the
Nymphs in a graceful dance; towards the end whereof,
Prospero starts suddenly, and speaks.*[115]

PROSPERO   [*aside:*] I had forgot that foul conspiracy
Of the beast Caliban and his confederates   140
Against my life: the minute of their plot
Is almost come. [*To the spirits:*] Well done! Avoid:
                                              no more.

*Juno and Ceres ascend in the chariot. To a strange, hollow
and confused noise, the other spirits gloomily vanish.*

FERDINAND This is strange: your father's in some passion
That works him strongly.

MIRANDA   Never till this day
Saw I him touched with anger so distempered.[116]

PROSPERO   You do look, my son, in a moved sort,
As if you were dismayed: be cheerful, sir.
Our revels now are ended. These our actors
(As I foretold you) were all spirits, and
Are melted into air, into thin air;   150

And, like the baseless fabric of this vision,
The cloud-capped towers, the gorgeous palaces,
The solemn temples, the great globe itself,
Yea, all which it inherit, shall dissolve,
And, like this insubstantial pageant faded,
Leave not a rack behind. We are such stuff
As dreams are made on; and our little life
Is rounded with a sleep. Sir, I am vexed.
Bear with my weakness; my old brain is troubled;
Be not disturbed with my infirmity.   160
If you be pleased, retire into my cell,
And there repose. A turn or two I'll walk,
To still my beating mind.

FERDINAND, MIRANDA   We wish your peace.
                        [*Exeunt Ferdinand and Miranda.*
PROSPERO   Come with a thought! I thank thee, Ariel: come![117]

                        Enter ARIEL.

ARIEL   Thy thoughts I cleave to. What's thy pleasure?
PROSPERO
                                                Spirit,
            We must prepare to meet with Caliban.
ARIEL   Ay, my commander; when I presented Ceres,[118]
            I thought to have told thee of it, but I feared
            Lest I might anger thee.
PROSPERO   Say again, where didst thou leave these varlets?   170
ARIEL   I told you, sir, they were red-hot with drinking;
            So full of valour, that they smote the air
            For breathing in their faces, beat the ground
            For kissing of their feet; yet always bending
            Towards their project. Then I beat my tabor,
            At which, like unbacked colts, they pricked their ears,
            Advanced their eyelids, lifted up their noses
            As they smelt music. So I charmed their ears
            That, calf-like, they my lowing followed, through
            Toothed briers, sharp furzes, pricking gorse,
                                    and thorns,   180
            Which entered their frail shins. At last I left them
            I'th' filthy mantled pool beyond your cell,
            There dancing up to th' chins, that the foul lake

O'er-stunk their feet.[119]

PROSPERO   This was well done, my bird.
Thy shape invisible retain thou still.
The trumpery in my house, go, bring it hither,
For stale to catch these thieves.

ARIEL   I go, I go.   [*Exit.*

PROSPERO   A devil, a born devil, on whose nature
Nurture can never stick; on whom my pains,
Humanely taken, all, all lost, quite lost;   190
And as with age his body uglier grows,
So his mind cankers. I will plague them all,
Even to roaring.

Enter ARIEL, *laden with glistering apparel,* &c.

                        Come, hang them on this line.

Prospero and Ariel remain, invisible to others.
Enter CALIBAN, STEPHANO *and* TRINCULO, *all wet.*

CALIBAN   Pray you, tread softly, that the blind mole may
Not hear a footfall: we now are near his cell.

STEPHANO   Monster, your fairy, which you say is a harmless fairy,
has done little better than played the Jack with us.

TRINCULO   Monster, I do smell all horse-piss, at which my nose is
in great indignation.

STEPHANO   So is mine. Do you hear, monster? If I should take a   200
displeasure against you, look you –

TRINCULO   Thou wert but a lost monster.

CALIBAN   Good my lord, give me thy favour still.
Be patient, for the prize I'll bring thee to
Shall hoodwink this mischance: therefore, speak
                                                          softly;
All's hushed as midnight yet.

TRINCULO   Ay, but to lose our bottles in the pool!

STEPHANO   There is not only disgrace and dishonour in that,
monster, but an infinite loss.

TRINCULO   That's more to me than my wetting; yet this is your   210
harmless fairy, monster.

STEPHANO   I will fetch off my bottle, though I be o'er ears for my
labour.

CALIBAN   Prithee, my king, be quiet. Seest thou here:

This is the mouth o'th' cell. No noise, and enter.
Do that good mischief which may make this island
Thine own for ever, and I, thy Caliban,
For aye thy foot-licker.

STEPHANO   Give me thy hand. I do begin to have bloody thoughts.

TRINCULO   O King Stephano, O peer! O worthy Stephano, look   220
what a wardrobe here is for thee![120]

CALIBAN   Let it alone, thou fool: it is but trash.

TRINCULO   O, ho, monster! We know what belongs to a frippery.
[*He tries on a gown.*] O King Stephano!

STEPHANO   Put off that gown, Trinculo. By this hand, I'll have that
gown.

TRINCULO   Thy grace shall have it.

CALIBAN   The dropsy drown this fool! What do you mean,
To dote thus on such luggage? Let't alone,
And do the murder first. If he awake,   230
From toe to crown he'll fill our skins with pinches,
Make us strange stuff.[121]

STEPHANO   Be you quiet, monster. – Mistress line, is not this my
jerkin? Now is the jerkin under the line: now, jerkin,
you are like to lose your hair, and prove a bald jerkin.[122]

TRINCULO   Do, do! We steal by line and level, an't like your grace.

STEPHANO   I thank thee for that jest; here's a garment for't. Wit
shall not go unrewarded while I am king of this country. 'Steal by line and level' is an excellent pass of pate;
there's another garment for't.   240

TRINCULO   Monster, come, put some lime upon your fingers,[123]
and away with the rest.

CALIBAN   I will have none on't: we shall lose our time,
And all be turned to barnacles, or to apes
With foreheads villainous low.

STEPHANO   Monster, lay-to your fingers: help to bear this away
where my hogshead of wine is, or I'll turn you out of
my kingdom. Go to, carry this.

TRINCULO   And this.

STEPHANO   Ay, and this.   250

They load Caliban with garments. A noise of hunters heard.
Enter divers SPIRITS, *in shape of dogs and hounds, hunting*
the trio; Prospero and Ariel setting them on.[124]

PROSPERO   Hey, Mountain, hey!

ARIEL   Silver: there it goes, Silver!

PROSPERO   Fury, Fury! There, Tyrant, there! Hark, hark!

        [*Exeunt Caliban, Stephano and Trinculo, pursued.*

Go, charge my goblins that they grind their joints
With dry convulsions, shorten up their sinews
With agèd cramps, and more pinch-spotted make them
Than pard or cat o' mountain.   [*Yells within.*

ARIEL   Hark, they roar.

PROSPERO   Let them be hunted soundly. At this hour
Lies at my mercy all mine enemies.
Shortly shall all my labours end, and thou   260
Shalt have the air at freedom. For a little,
Follow, and do me service.

                                    [*Exeunt.*

ACT 5, SCENE I.

Before Prospero's cell.

Enter PROSPERO*, in his magic robes, and* ARIEL.

PROSPERO　Now does my project gather to a head:
My charms crack not, my spirits obey, and Time
Goes upright with his carriage. How's the day?

ARIEL　On the sixth hour, at which time, my lord,
You said our work should cease.[125]

PROSPERO　　　　　　　　　　　　　I did say so
When first I raised the tempest. Say, my spirit,
How fares the King and's followers?

ARIEL　　　　　　　　　　　　　Confined together
In the same fashion as you gave in charge,
Just as you left them: all prisoners, sir,
In the line-grove which weather-fends your cell:　　　10
They cannot budge till your release. The King,
His brother, and yours, abide all three distracted,
And the remainder mourning over them,
Brimful of sorrow and dismay; but chiefly
Him you termed, sir, 'the good old lord, Gonzalo'.
His tears run down his beard like winter's drops
From eaves of reeds. Your charm so strongly
　　　　　　　　　　　　　　　works 'em
That, if you now beheld them, your affections
Would become tender.

PROSPERO　　　　　　　　　Dost thou think so, spirit?

ARIEL　Mine would, sir, were I human.

PROSPERO　　　　　　　　　　　　And mine shall.　　20
Hast thou (which art but air) a touch, a feeling
Of their afflictions, and shall not myself,
One of their kind, that relish all as sharply
Passion as they,[126] be kindlier moved than thou art?
Though with their high wrongs I am struck to
　　　　　　　　　　　　　　　th' quick,
Yet, with my nobler reason, 'gainst my fury
Do I take part: the rarer action is

In virtue than in vengeance:[127] they being penitent,
The sole drift of my purpose doth extend
Not a frown further. Go, release them, Ariel.   30
My charms I'll break, their senses I'll restore,
And they shall be themselves.

ARIEL   I'll fetch them, sir. [*Exit.*

Prospero draws a large horizontal circle with his staff.[128]

PROSPERO   Ye elves of hills, brooks, standing lakes and groves,
And ye, that on the sands with printless foot
Do chase the ebbing Neptune, and do fly him
When he comes back; you demi-puppets that
By moonshine do the green sour ringlets make,
Whereof the ewe not bites; and you, whose pastime
Is to make midnight mushrumps, that rejoice
To hear the solemn curfew;[129] by whose aid   40
(Weak masters though ye be)[130] I have bedimmed
The noontide sun, called forth the mutinous winds,
And 'twixt the green sea and the azured vault
Set roaring war: to the dread rattling thunder
Have I given fire, and rifted Jove's stout oak
With his own bolt; the strong-based promontory
Have I made shake, and by the spurs plucked up
The pine and cedar; graves at my command
Have waked their sleepers, oped, and let 'em forth
By my so potent art.[131] But this rough magic   50
I here abjure; and when I have required
Some heavenly music (which even now I do)
To work mine end upon their senses that
This airy charm is for, I'll break my staff,
Bury it certain fathoms in the earth,
And deeper than did ever plummet sound
I'll drown my book.   [*Solemn music.*

Here enters ARIEL *before; then* ALONSO, *with a frantic gesture, attended
by* GONZALO; SEBASTIAN *and* ANTONIO *in like manner, attended by*
ADRIAN *and* FRANCISCO: *they all enter the circle which Prospero had
made, and there stand charmed; which Prospero observing, speaks.*[132]

[*To Alonso:*] A solemn air, and the best comforter
To an unsettled fancy, cure thy brains

(Now useless), boiled within thy skull.[133]
[*To Sebastian and Antonio:*]   There stand,   60
For you are spell-stopped.[134] –
Holy Gonzalo, honourable man,
Mine eyes, ev'n sociable to the show of thine,
Fall fellowly drops. [*Aside:*] The charm dissolves apace;
And as the morning steals upon the night,
Melting the darkness, so their rising senses
Begin to chase the ignorant fumes that mantle
Their clearer reason.[135] – O good Gonzalo,
My true preserver, and a loyal sir
To him thou follow'st: I will pay thy graces   70
Home,[136] both in word and deed. – Most cruelly
Didst thou, Alonso, use me and my daughter.
Thy brother was a furtherer in the act; –
Thou art pinched for't now, Sebastian.
[*To Antonio:*]   Flesh and blood,
You, brother mine, that entertained ambition,
Expelled remorse and nature; who, with Sebastian
(Whose inward pinches therefore are most strong),
Would here have killed your king: I do forgive thee,
Unnatural though thou art. [*Aside:*] Their understanding
Begins to swell, and the approaching tide   80
Will shortly fill the reasonable shore
That now lies foul and muddy. Not one of them
That yet looks on me, or would know me. – Ariel,
Fetch me the hat and rapier in my cell.   [*Exit Ariel.*
l will discase me, and myself present
As I was sometime Millaine. Quickly, spirit!
Thou shalt ere long be free.

Returning, ARIEL *sings, and helps to attire him.*

ARIEL   Where the bee sucks, there suck I:
                          In a cowslip's bell I lie;
                          There I couch, when owls do cry.   90
                          On the bat's back I do fly
                          After summer merrily.
                    Merrily, merrily, shall I live now,
                    Under the blossom that hangs on the bough.

PROSPERO   Why, that's my dainty Ariel! I shall miss thee,
            But yet thou shalt have freedom. – So, so, so.[137] –
            To the King's ship, invisible as thou art;
            There shalt thou find the mariners asleep
            Under the hatches. The master and the boatswain
            Being awake, enforce them to this place;   100
            And presently, I prithee.

ARIEL   I drink the air before me, and return
            Or ere your pulse twice beat.   [Exit.

GONZALO   All torment, trouble, wonder and amazement
            Inhabits here: some heavenly power guide us
            Out of this fearful country!

PROSPERO   Behold, sir King,
            The wrongèd Duke of Millaine, Prospero:
            For more assurance that a living prince
            Does now speak to thee, I embrace thy body,
            And to thee and thy company I bid   110
            A hearty welcome.

ALONSO   Whe'er thou be'st he or no,
            Or some enchanted trifle to abuse me,
            As late I have been, I not know. Thy pulse
            Beats, as of flesh and blood; and, since I saw thee,
            Th'affliction of my mind amends, with which
            I fear a madness held me. This must crave –
            And if this be at all – a most strange story.
            Thy dukedom I resign,[138] and do entreat
            Thou pardon me my wrongs. But how
                                        should Prospero
            Be living, and be here?

PROSPERO   [to Gonzalo:]   First, noble friend,   120
            Let me embrace thine age, whose honour cannot
            Be measured or confined.

GONZALO   Whether this be,
            Or be not, I'll not swear.

PROSPERO   You do yet taste
            Some subtleties o'th'isle, that will not let you
            Believe things certain. – Welcome, my friends all!
            [Aside to Sebastian and Antonio:]
            But you, my brace of lords: were I so minded,

I here could pluck his Highness' frown upon you,
And justify you traitors. At this time
I will tell no tales.

SEBASTIAN [*aside:*]   The devil speaks in him.

PROSPERO   No. –
For you (most wicked sir), whom to call brother   130
Would even infect my mouth, I do forgive
Thy rankest fault – all of them; and require
My dukedom of thee, which perforce, I know,
Thou must restore.

ALONSO   If thou beest Prospero,
Give us particulars of thy preservation,
How thou hast met us here, who three hours since
Were wracked upon this shore; where I have lost
(How sharp the point of this remembrance is!)
My dear son Ferdinand.

PROSPERO   I am woe for't, sir.

ALONSO Irreparable is the loss, and patience   140
Says it is past her cure.

PROSPERO   I rather think
You have not sought her help, of whose soft grace
For the like loss I have her sovereign aid,
And rest myself content.

ALONSO   You the like loss?

PROSPERO As great to me as late; and, supportable
To make the dear loss, have I means much weaker
Than you may call to comfort you; for I
Have lost my daughter.[139]

ALONSO   A daughter?
O heavens, that they were living both in Naples,
The king and queen there! That they were, I wish   150
Myself were mudded in that oozy bed
Where my son lies. When did you lose your
                                      daughter?

PROSPERO In this last tempest. I perceive these lords
At this encounter do so much admire,
That they devour their reason, and scarce think
Their eyes do offices of truth, their words
Are natural breath.[140] But, howsoe'er you have

Been justled from your senses, know for certain
That I am Prospero and that very Duke
Which was thrust forth of Millaine, who most strangely   160
Upon this shore (where you were wracked) was
                             landed,
To be the lord on't. No more yet of this,
For 'tis a chronicle of day by day,[141]
Not a relation for a breakfast, nor
Befitting this first meeting. Welcome, sir.
This cell's my court: here have I few attendants,
And subjects none abroad. Pray you, look in.
My dukedom since you have given me again,
I will requite you with as good a thing:
At least, bring forth a wonder, to content ye   170
As much as me my dukedom.

Here Prospero discovers FERDINAND *and* MIRANDA, *playing at chess.*[142]

MIRANDA   Sweet lord, you play me false.
FERDINAND   My dearest love,
I would not for the world.
MIRANDA   Yes, for a score of kingdoms you should wrangle,
And I would call it fair play.[143]
ALONSO   If this prove
A vision of the island, one dear son
Shall I twice lose.
SEBASTIAN   A most high miracle!
FERDINAND   *[emerging:]* Though the seas threaten, they are merciful;
I have cursed them without cause.   *[He kneels.*
ALONSO   Now all the blessings
Of a glad father compass thee about!   180
Arise, and say how thou cam'st here.   *[Ferdinand rises.*
MIRANDA   O wonder!
How many goodly creatures are there here!
How beauteous mankind is! O brave new world,
That has such people in't!
PROSPERO   'Tis new to thee.
ALONSO   What is this maid, with whom thou wast at play?
Your eld'st acquaintance cannot be three hours.
Is she the goddess that hath severed us,

And brought us thus together?

FERDINAND　　　　　　　　　　　Sir, she is mortal;
But, by immortal Providence, she's mine.
I chose her when I could not ask my father　　　　190
For his advice, nor thought I had one. She
Is daughter to this famous Duke of Millaine,
Of whom so often I have heard renown,
But never saw before; of whom I have
Received a second life; and second father
This lady makes him to me.

ALONSO　　　　　　　　　　　　　I am hers.[144]
But O, how oddly will it sound, that I
Must ask my child forgiveness!

PROSPERO　　　　　　　　　　　　There, sir, stop.
Let us not burden our remembrance with
A heaviness that's gone.

GONZALO　　　　　　　　　　　　I have inly wept,　　　　200
Or should have spoke ere this. Look down, you gods,
And on this couple drop a blessèd crown;
For it is you that have chalked forth the way
Which brought us hither.

ALONSO　　　　　　　　　　　I say 'Amen', Gonzalo.

GONZALO　Was Millaine thrust from Millaine, that his issue
Should become kings of Naples? O, rejoice
Beyond a common joy; and set it down
With gold on lasting pillars: in one voyage
Did Claribel her husband find at Tunis,
And Ferdinand, her brother, found a wife　　　　210
Where he himself was lost, Prospero his dukedom
In a poor isle, and all of us ourselves
When no man was his own.[145]

ALONSO　[to Ferdinand and Miranda:]　Give me your hands.
Let grief and sorrow still embrace his heart
That doth not wish you joy.

GONZALO　　　　　　　　　　　　Be it so. Amen.

Enter ARIEL, with the MASTER and BOATSWAIN amazedly following.[146]

O look sir, look sir, here is more of us!
I prophesied, if a gallows were on land,

This fellow could not drown. [*To the Boatswain:*]
                         Now, Blasphemy,
That swear'st grace o'erboard: not an oath on shore?
Has thou no mouth by land?[147] What is the news?   220

BOATSWAIN The best news is that we have safely found
Our king and company. The next, our ship,
Which but three glasses since we gave out split,
Is tight and yare and bravely rigged as when
We first put out to sea.

ARIEL   [*aside to Prospero:*]   Sir, all this service
Have I done since I went.

PROSPERO   [*aside to Ariel:*]   My tricksy spirit!

ALONSO These are not natural events; they strengthen
From strange to stranger. Say, how came you hither?

BOATSWAIN If I did think, sir, I were well awake,
I'd strive to tell you. We were dead of sleep,   230
And (how, we know not) all clapped under hatches,
Where, but even now, with strange and several noises
Of roaring, shrieking, howling, jingling chains,
And mo diversity of sounds, all horrible,
We were awaked; straightway at liberty;
Where we, in all our trim,[148] freshly beheld
Our royal, good, and gallant ship; our master
Cap'ring to eye her. On a trice, so please you,
Even in a dream, were we divided from them,
And were brought moping hither.[149]

ARIEL   [*aside to Prospero:*]   Was't well done?   240

PROSPERO   [*aside to him:*] Bravely, my diligence; thou shalt be free.

ALONSO This is as strange a maze as e'er men trod.
And there is in this business more than nature
Was ever conduct of. Some oracle
Must rectify our knowledge.

PROSPERO   Sir, my liege,
Do not infest your mind with beating on
The strangeness of this business. At picked leisure
(Which shall be shortly single), I'll resolve you,
Which to you shall seem probable, of every
These happened accidents.[150] Till when, be cheerful   250

And think of each thing well. [*Aside to Ariel:*]
                     Come hither, spirit.
Set Caliban and his companions free:
Untie the spell.   [*Exit Ariel.*
[*To Alonso:*]   How fares my gracious sir?
There are yet missing of your company
Some few odd lads that you remember not.

Enter ARIEL, *driving in* CALIBAN, STEPHANO *and*
       TRINCULO *in their stolen apparel.*

STEPHANO Every man shift for all the rest, and let no man take
care for himself; for all is but fortune. Coragio, bully-
monster, coragio![151]

TRINCULO If these be true spies which I wear in my head, here's a
goodly sight.   260

CALIBAN O Setebos, these be brave spirits indeed!
How fine my master is! I am afraid
He will chastise me.

SEBASTIAN Ha, ha!
What things are these, my lord Antonio?
Will money buy 'em?

ANTONIO   Very like: one of them
Is a plain fish, and no doubt marketable.

PROSPERO Mark but the badges of these men, my lords,
Then say if they be true.[152] This mis-shapen knave:
His mother was a witch, and one so strong   270
That could control the moon, make flows and ebbs,
And deal in her command without her power.[153]
These three have robbed me, and this demi-devil
(For he's a bastard one) had plotted with them
To take my life. Two of these fellows you
Must know and own; this thing of darkness I
Acknowledge mine.

CALIBAN   I shall be pinched to death.

ALONSO Is not this Stephano, my drunken butler?

SEBASTIAN He is drunk now; where had he wine?

ALONSO And Trinculo is reeling-ripe: where should they   280
Find this grand liquor that hath gilded 'em?
[*To Trinculo:*] How cam'st thou in this pickle?

TRINCULO	I have been in such a pickle since I saw you last that, I
	fear me, will never out of my bones: I shall not fear fly-
	blowing.[154]
SEBASTIAN	Why, how now, Stephano?
STEPHANO	O touch me not: I am not Stephano, but a cramp.
PROSPERO	You'd be king o'th'isle, sirrah?
STEPHANO	I should have been a sore one then.
ALONSO	[indicating Caliban:]

290

ALONSO
This is a strange thing as e'er I looked on.

PROSPERO He is as disproportioned in his manners
As in his shape. [To Caliban:] Go, sirrah, to my cell;
Take with you your companions; as you look
To have my pardon, trim it handsomely.

CALIBAN Ay, that I will; and I'll be wise hereafter,
And seek for grace. What a thrice-double ass
Was I, to take this drunkard for a god,
And worship this dull fool!

PROSPERO   Go to, away.

ALONSO [to Stephano and Trinculo:]
Hence, and bestow your luggage where you found it.

SEBASTIAN Or stole it rather.

300

                    [Exeunt Caliban, Stephano and Trinculo.

PROSPERO [to Alonso:] Sir, I invite your Highness and your train
To my poor cell, where you shall take your rest
For this one night; which, part of it, I'll waste
With such discourse as, I not doubt, shall make it
Go quick away: the story of my life,
And the particular accidents gone by
Since I came to this isle. And in the morn
I'll bring you to your ship, and so to Naples,
Where I have hope to see the nuptial
Of these our dear-belov'd solemnizèd;[155]

310

And thence retire me to my Millaine, where
Every third thought shall be my grave.[156]

ALONSO   I long
To hear the story of your life, which must
Take the ear strangely.

PROSPERO   I'll deliver all;
And promise you calm seas, auspicious gales,

And sail so expeditious that shall catch
Your royal fleet far off.[157] – My Ariel, chick,
That is thy charge; then to the elements
Be free, and fare thou well.   [*Exit Ariel.*
                          – Please you, draw near.
                             [*Exeunt all but Prospero.*

EPILOGUE,

spoken by PROSPERO.[158]

Now my charms are all o'erthrown,
And what strength I have's mine own,
Which is most faint. Now, 'tis true,
I must be here confined by you,
Or sent to Naples. Let me not,
Since I have my dukedom got,
And pardoned the deceiver, dwell
In this bare island, by your spell;
But release me from my bands,
With the help of your good hands.   10
Gentle breath of yours my sails
Must fill, or else my project fails,
Which was to please. Now I want
Spirits to enforce, art to enchant;
And my ending is despair,
Unless I be relieved by prayer
Which pierces so, that it assaults
Mercy itself, and frees all faults.[159]
As you from crimes would pardoned be,
Let your indulgence set me free.   20

                                            [*Exit.*

NOTES ON *THE TEMPEST*

In these notes, the following abbreviations are used:

e.g.: *exempli gratia* (Latin): for example.

Essayes *The Essayes or Morall, Politike and Millitarie Discourses of Lo: Michaell de Montaigne*, translated by John Florio (London: Edward Blount, 1603).

FI: First Folio (1623).

Falconer: Alexander F. Falconer: *Shakespeare and the Sea* (London: Constable, 1964).

Florio: John Florio: *Queen Anna's New World of Words, or Dictionarie of the Italian and English Tongues* (London: Edward Blount and William Barret, 1611).

i.e.: *id est* (Latin): that is.

Kermode: *The Tempest*, ed. Frank Kermode (London: Methuen, 1964).

O.E.D.: *The Oxford English Dictionary* (2nd edn.: Oxford: Oxford University Press, 1989).

Orgel: *The Tempest*, ed. Stephen Orgel (Oxford and New York: Oxford University Press, 1987; reprinted, 1994).

Ovid: *The XV. Bookes of P. Ouidius Naso, Entituled, Metamorphoses*, tr. Arthur Golding (London, 1603).

S.D.: stage-direction.

Wilson: *The Tempest*, ed. Sir Arthur Quiller-Couch and John Dover Wilson (London: Cambridge University Press, 1921; reprinted, 1957).

Biblical quotations are from the Geneva Bible.

Where a pun or an ambiguity is glossed, the meanings are distinguished as (a) and (b); otherwise, differing meanings are distinguished as (i) and (ii).

1 (1.1: S.D.) A tempestuous . . . heard: This wording corresponds to that of the First Folio (F1).

2 (1.1: S.D. after line 4) Enter MARINERS: F1 marks no specific
exeunt for them before their later re-entry. They may come
and go (in ones, twos or groups) during the scene.

3 (1.1.12) bosun?:   Here F1 has the spelling 'Boson', though
elsewhere the word is spelt in full as 'Boteswaine'. The word
means 'foreman of the crew'.

4 (1.1.16–17) What cares . . . king?:   F1 gives the singular verb
with the plural subject. The play offers several other examples
(e.g. at 1.2.482, 4.1.259, 5.1.7 and 5.1.216).

5 (1.1.27–8) his . . . gallows: alluding to the proverb, 'He that is
born to be hanged shall never be drowned'.

6 (1.1.32–3) Down . . . main-course: 'Lower the topmast! Quick!
Lower, lower! Using the mainsail, seek to steer towards open
water.' (See Falconer, p. 37.) A topmast is normally fixed to
the top of the lower mast.

7 (1.1.46–7) Lay her a-hold! . . . Lay her off!:   Possibly: 'Bring
the ship close to the wind (more obliquely to the wind-
direction) by setting the foresail in addition to the mainsail, in
the hope of reaching the open sea.' (See Falconer, pp. 38–9.)

8 (1.1.53–4) lie . . . tides: Pirates were sometimes punished by
being hanged at low-water mark and left there until three
tides had immersed them.

9 (1.1.56: S.D) VOICES WITHIN: F1 reads 'A confused noyse within'.

10 (1.1.61) long heath, brown furze: 'heather and parched gorse'.
F1 has 'Long heath, Browne firrs'. As furze is not normally
brown, some editors convert 'Browne firs' to 'broom, furze';
but 'Browne' may simply mean 'dried-up'. (Another possible
reading takes 'Long heath' and 'Browne firs' to mean 'barren
heath-land' and 'brown fir-trees'; while yet another treats
'Long' as a misreading of 'ling'.)

11 (1.2: S.D.) PROSPERO . . MIRANDA: Florio states that 'Prospero'
means 'prosperous, successfull, thriving, luckie, happie, fortunate.
Also healthie and strong, or sound and lustie'. 'Miranda' means '[a
female who is] admirable, to be wondered at'.

12 (1.2.1) *art*:   The term is repeatedly used in the play to mean 'magic', but it has wide connotations.

13 (1.2.29) *no soul* – :   Anacoluthon (breach of syntax) occurs here: the sense requires an additional word (e.g. 'perished').

14 (1.2.58) *Millaine*:   I preserve the spelling of F1. The word (unlike 'Milan', its modern equivalent) is stressed on the first syllable.

15 (1.2.59) *a princess*:   F1 has 'And Princesse'. Some editors preserve the 'And'; others regard it as a misprint.

16 (1.2.73) *the liberal arts*:   grammar, logic, rhetoric, arithmetic, geometry, music and astronomy.

17 (1.2.92) *O'er-prized . . . rate*:   'exceeded the common people's understanding' (Orgel).

18 (1.2.94) *Like . . . parent*: alluding to the proverbial notion that good fathers often have inferior sons.

19 (1.2.100–102) *having . . . lie*:   The probable sense is: 'having made of his memory such a sinner against truth as to believe his own lie in the act of telling it'. Taking 'unto' as 'against' is, however, a rather strained reading; F1 has 'into', not 'unto'; and Wilson emends 'into' as 'minted' (i.e. 'coined').

20 (1.2.103–5) *out . . . prerogative*:   'as a consequence of taking my place and accomplishing the manifestations of dukedom with all its powers'.

21 (1.2.118–19) *I should . . . grandmother*:   'It would be sinful of me not to hold my grandmother in high esteem' (i.e. 'I must not think that my grandmother committed adultery, even though that would account for the difference between my good father and his wicked brother').

22 (1.2.159) *By Providence divine.*:   In F1, this phrase concludes with a comma. I follow various editors in using a full stop here; but the phrase also makes good sense if it ends with a comma or with no punctuation, so that divine Providence is then implicit in the food and water supplied by Gonzalo.

23 (1.2.172–3) *made . . . can*:   'made you gain more than can other princesses'. F1 has 'Princesse', which may also (as Orgel suggests) be a spelling of 'princes', a generic term for royal children of either sex.

24 (1.2.188) *Ariel*: Though his name suggests the aërial, Prospero's Ariel is associated with all four elements: fire, air, water and (at line 255) earth. Literally, the name means 'Lion of God'; in Isaiah 29:1 it refers to Jerusalem; and it was sometimes applied to a spirit of earth (not air) or even a devil.

25 (1.2.196–206) *I boarded . . . shake*: The idea of a ship beset by fire during a thunderstorm may have been suggested by reports of 'St Elmo's Fire', an electrical 'brush discharge' which makes parts of a vessel glow and shimmer with flickering brightness. (Falconer, p. 40, praises Shakespeare's visual accuracy.)

26 (1.2.212) *afire . . . Ferdinand*: F1 has no punctuation between 'me' and 'the'. Wilson follows F1, thinking that Ferdinand is indeed 'afire'. Other editors punctuate so as to suggest that only the vessel displays Ariel's flames.

27 (1.2.239–41) *Past . . . preciously*: 'Two glasses' means two hours past noon, so the time must be past 2 p.m.. Prospero's plan requires less than four hours for its completion: an unusually taut time-scheme for a Shakespearian play.

28 (1.2.258–9) *The foul witch Sycorax . . . hoop*: Sycorax may be a version of 'Stycorax': 'Hateful Old Raven', or, more freely, 'Nasty Old Crow'. The Greek word *stygnos* (like the name of the underworld river Styx) means 'hateful' or 'gloomy', and *korax* is Greek for 'raven', a bird of ill-omen associated with witchcraft. Shakespeare's Sycorax is based partly on the description of the enchantress Medea in Ovid's *Metamorphoses*, Book 7.

29 (1.2.266–7) *for one . . . life*: The 'one thing she did' is probably her becoming pregnant. (Hence, perhaps, 'blue-eyed' in line 269, for pregnant women sometimes have bluish eyelids. A possible emendation is 'blear-eyed'.)

30 (1.2.301–5) *Go . . . diligence*: In F1, this passage reads:

> Goe make thy selfe like a Nymph o'th'Sea,
> Be subiect to no sight but thine, and mine: inuisible
> To euery eye-ball else: goe take this shape
> And hither come in't: goe: hence
> With diligence.

The text here is irregular and seems corrupt. The first and fourth of these lines are metrically too short; the second is too long. My emendation reduces the irregularity. I preserve the short line 'With diligence' in order to retain a rhyming conclusion.

31 (1.2.320–21) *got . . . dam*:   witches were supposed to copulate with the devil.

32 (1.2.327–9) *urchins . . . thee*:   'hedgehogs will all exercise their prickly spines on you during that extent of night in which they may go to work'. F1 has 'Vrchins / Shall for that vast of night, that they may worke / All exercise on thee'. Some editors emend the phrasing thus: 'Urchins / Shall forth at vast of night, that they may work / All exercise on thee'.

33 (1.2.332) *This . . . mother*:   Normally, as Edmund in *King Lear* knew, a claim to ownership by inheritance was invalid if the claimant was born illegitimately.

34 (1.2.336–7) *the bigger . . . night*:   Genesis 1:16 states: 'God then made two great lightes: the greater light to rule the daie, and the lesse light to rule the night . . . '

35 (1.2.367–8) *be quick . . . business*:   'you had better be prompt to perform other tasks'.

36 (1.2.378–9) *Curtsied . . . whist)*:   'when you have curtseyed and kissed (the wild waves being stilled)'. Editors punctuate this variously. Orgel preserves the F1 punctuation and reads thus: 'Curtsied when you have, and kissed / The wild waves whist,'. He takes the meaning to be either 'kissed the wild waves into silence' (which seems unlikely) or 'kissed (each other) until the wild waves are silent'. One of Shakespeare's sources, Golding's translation of Ovid's *Metamorphoses*, uses 'whist' to mean 'stilled': 'The moysting Ayre was whist[:] no leafe ye could haue mouing seene' (Bk. 7, line 253).

37 (1.2.382) *The burthen*:   The 'burthen' is the refrain or chorus. Editions vary considerably in their allocation of the refrain. Some give the repeated 'Bow-wow' and 'Cockadiddle-dow' to the spirits. F1 places after the words '*the burthen.*' the direction 'Burthen dispersedly.', followed by '*Harke, harke, bowgh wawgh: the watch-Dogges barke, / bowgh-wawgh.*', and allocates the remaining words of the song to Ariel. My arrangement follows F1 closely.

38 (1.2.412–13) *The fringèd . . . yond*: 'Open your lash-fringed
eyelids, and tell me what you see over there.' The implication
is that Prospero has magically put Miranda into an entranced
slumber since the departure of Caliban, and is now awakening
her.

39 (1.2.425–7) *Most . . . island*: 'You are surely the goddess
served by these melodies! Grant my prayer to know whether
you are a resident of this island'. (In Virgil's *Aeneid*, Bk. 1, the
goddess Venus, in the guise of a maiden huntress, approaches
Aeneas, and he exclaims: 'Goddess! For a goddess surely you
must be.')

40 (1.2.430) *O you wonder!*: Unwittingly, he is punning on
Miranda's name, rather as Juliet had unwittingly punned on
Romeo's when first addressing him. ('Admired Miranda!', at
3.1.37, maintains such wit.)

41 (1.2.433–4) *I am . . . spoken*: He assumes that his father has
died and that he himself is now King of Naples.

42 (1.2.442) *his . . . twain*: This 'brave son' does not appear in
the play, being perhaps a relic of an earlier draft or an uncut
version.

43 (1.2.470: S.D) *He . . . magic*: In F1, the direction is: '*He
drawes, and is charmed from mouing.*'

44 (1.2.473) *My foot my tutor?*: 'Does the lowest part of me (my
offspring) presume to instruct me?'

45 (1.2.492) *nor this man's threats*: F1's 'nor' may be erroneous;
the intended sense is 'and also the threats of this man'.

46 (2.1.10) *He . . . porridge*: Alonso has said 'peace', so Sebastian
puns on 'pease porridge' (a thick pea-soup).

47 (2.1.16–20) *When . . . purposed*: The pun on 'entertainer'
(first meaning 'accommodator' but suggesting to Sebastian
'performer') leads to the counter-pun on 'dollar' (payment) of
'dolour' (sadness).

48 (2.1.29–32) *The old . . . laughter*: The 'old cock' is Gonzalo;
the 'cockerel' is Adrian. Antonio (recalling the proverb 'He
laughs that wins') says that the winner of the bet will gain
laughter; and 'laughter' could also mean a batch of eggs, thus
sustaining the metaphor.

49 (2.1.72, 75, 78) *widow Dido . . . 'widower Aeneas' . . . Tunis*:
Virgil's *Aeneid* tells how Aeneas (whose wife, Creusa, had
died) reached North Africa after a supernaturally-ordained
shipwreck. There, he became the lover of Dido, Queen of
Carthage, the widow of Sychaeus. Aeneas eventually deserted
her, and she committed suicide. Modern Tunis lies about 11
miles west of the site of ancient Carthage. (Antonio mocks the
notion that Dido, the legendary love-lorn queen, should be
summed up in the demeaning jingle, 'widow Dido'. Wilson,
p. 95, suggests that he pronounces it 'widdow Diddo'.)

50 (2.1.82–4) *His word . . . too*:   The legendary Amphion played
his lyre so movingly that stones moved to form the walls of
Thebes. Antonio and Sebastian jest that Gonzalo is even more
amazing: his words build, at the location of Tunis, the houses
as well as the walls of Carthage.

51 (2.1.99–100) *in a sort . . . fished for*:   By 'in a sort', Gonzalo
means 'in a sense (not fresh like a newly-caught fish)';
Antonio, while punning on 'sort', which could mean 'item
drawn at a lottery', suggests that it is indeed like a newly-
caught fish.

52 (2.1.102–3) *You cram . . . sense*:   'You cram your words into
my ears, but I cannot stomach your attempted consolation.'
(The image relates to that of a goose being force-fed.)

53 (2.1.125–7) *the fair soul . . . bow*:   (a) 'her beautiful spirit, like
a set of scales, weighed distaste on one side and obedience on
the other, to see which should descend'; (b) 'her beautiful
spirit weighed up the choice between distaste and obedience,
pondering which she should respect'. (Some editions take F1's
'should' to be a compression of 'she should'; and 'bow' could
mean either 'descend' or 'make obeisance to'.)

54 (2.1.138) *Fowl weather?*:   Sebastian had earlier described
Gonzalo as the 'old cock'; hence (probably) the pun.

55 (2.1.143–59) *I'th' commonwealth . . . people*:   This passage derives from Montaigne's essay, 'Of the Caniballes', in the
translation by John Florio (1603). In line 143, 'by contraries'
means 'in a manner contrary to what is usual'; in 144, 'traffic'
means 'commerce'; and, in 158, 'it' means 'its'. Montaigne

(*Essayes*, Bk. 1, Chap. 30) says of the indigenous people of America:

> It is a nation . . . that hath no kinde of traffike, no knowledge of Letters, no intelligence of numbers, no name of magistrate, nor of politike superioritie; no vse of service, of riches or of poverty; no contracts, no successions, no dividences, no occupation but idle; no respect of kindred, but common, no apparrell but naturall, no manuring of lands, no vse of wine, corne, or mettle. The very words that import lying, falshood, treason, dissimulation, covetousnes, envie, detraction, and pardon, were never heard of amongst-them.

56 (2.1.163) *Golden Age*:   The mythical Golden Age, as described in Ovid's *Metamorphoses*, was an era of virtue, peace and plenty, when no laws or penalties were needed, and the earth produced crops spontaneously.

57 (2.1.163) *God save his Majesty!*:   F1 has "Saue his Maiesty.' A 1606 Statute against oaths may have resulted in the omission of 'God' before 'saue' (save). Restoration of 'God' reduces the irregularity of the metre.

58 (2.1.175–7) *you would . . . changing*:   'if the moon kept still for five weeks (which is impossible), you would steal her from the crystalline sphere in which she is supposed to be fixed': i.e. 'you are arrogantly ineffectual'.

59 (2.1.178) *We . . . a-batfowling*:   'We would indeed, and then proceed to trap gullible fools (like yourself).'

60 (2.1.200) *th'occasion speaks thee*:   'opportunity calls you'. Some editors punctuate this line as 'What thou shouldst be th'occasion speaks thee, and' (i.e. 'The opportunity reveals to you what you should be, and').

61 (2.1.214–16) *Trebles . . . me*:   'Trebles thee o'er' means 'makes you thrice greater'. 'Standing water' means 'waiting to move'. Sebastian replies to Antonio by saying that heredity (by making him a younger son who is slothful) inclines him to shrink from opportunities of advancement.

62 (2.1.225–9) *Although . . . persuade)*:   'Although Gonzalo, this forgetful lord, who will soon be forgotten when he is buried, has here almost persuaded (because he's a devil for persuasion, indeed it's his sole vocation)' . . .

63 (2.1.234–6) *even . . . there*: (perhaps:) 'ambition itself cannot glimpse further, but doubts that anything more is to be discovered'. Some editors read 'douts' (douses) instead of 'doubts'.

64 (2.1.240) *Ten . . . life*: 'thirty miles further away than a man can travel in a lifetime'.

65 (2.1.243) *she that from whom*: 'on the journey away from whom'.

66 (2.1.259–60) *I myself . . . chat*: 'I could teach a jackdaw to converse as profoundly as he does.'

67 (2.1.273–4) *candied . . . molest!*: 'let them be turned to sugary confections and melt away before troubling me!' In Shakespeare's works, a famous recurrent associative cluster links falsehood and treachery with dissolving sweets. (In *Antony and Cleopatra*, Act 4, scene 12, false followers 'do discandy, melt their sweets'.)

68 (2.2.52) *a tailor . . . itch*: Orgel (p. 146) remarks that tailors were deemed unmanly. In addition, however, Stephano is punning: a tailor might be a person familiar with 'tails' (buttocks and genital areas): see *A Midsummer Night's Dream*, 2.1.54.

69 (2.2.59–60) *As proper . . . four legs*: He adapts the cliché, 'As good a man as ever went on two legs.'

70 (2.2.74–5) *I will . . . him*: 'no sum paid to me for him will be too high'.

71 (2.2.79–80) *that . . . cat*: He recalls the proverbial 'liquor that would make a cat speak'.

72 (2.2.95) *I have . . . spoon*: Proverbial: 'He must have a long spoon that will eat with the devil.'

73 (2.2.125) *kiss the book*: Traditionally, a person kissed the Bible to confirm an oath.

74 (2.2.135) *thee . . . bush*: The man in the moon was supposed to own a dog and carry a bush.

75 (2.2.166) *scamels*: perhaps the small fish described in French as *fort scameux* (very scaly). F1 has 'Scamels'. Editors have postulated various emendations, e.g. 'seamells' or 'seamews' (i.e. gulls), and 'staniels' or 'stannels' (kestrels).

76 (3.1.1–2) *their labour . . . off*:   probably: 'taking pleasure in them compensates for their laboriousness'.

77 (3.1.12–13) *such baseness . . . executor*:   'such a base task was never undertaken by anyone comparable [i.e. so noble]'.

78 (3.1.14–15) *these . . . do it*:   'my pleasant thoughts of Miranda lighten my work: when I toil, they are most actively present'. Where F1 has 'busie lest', Kermode's emendation 'busil'est' (most busily) seems plausible.

79 (3.1.46) *put it to the foil*:   foiled it; subjected her finest quality, as if a jewel were marred by its setting instead of being enhanced by it.

80 (3.2.58) *knock . . . head*:   a biblical method of murder (see Judges 4:21 and 5:26), using a very long nail or spike.

81 (3.2.102) *king*:   Aptly and ironically, 'Stephano' means 'crown'. Later, Caliban will call Stephano 'my king', and Trinculo will call him 'King Stephano'.

82 (3.2.146) *I'll follow Stephano*:   F1 has 'Ile follow *Stephano.*' Some editors insert a comma after 'follow', but F1 makes good sense: Caliban leads, Stephano follows him, and Trinculo prudently goes last.

83 (3.3: S.D. after 17) Solemn . . . on the top (invisible):   This direction corresponds to part of that in F1. In the theatre, the musicians play in a gallery above the stage, and Prospero thus appears to be located in an even higher gallery. He is 'invisible' to the castaways but obviously not to the audience.

84 (3.3: S.D. after 19) Enter . . . depart: The phrasing corresponds to that in F1, though F1 locates this direction as a continuation of that following line 17.

85 (3.3.21–4) *A living . . . there*:   'A living drollery' may mean 'a real-life comedy' or 'an animated caricature'. The mythical phoenix was unique: it nested in a single tree, and was reborn from the ashes of its own funeral pyre.

86 (3.3.26–7) *Travellers . . . 'em*:   'Travellers' tales are true, even though they are denounced by foolish people who do not travel.'

87 (3.3.39) *Praise in departing*:   proverbial, meaning 'Wait till the end before you give praise'.

88 (3.3.46–7) *men . . . breasts?*:   Such men were described by Pliny the Elder in *Historia Naturalis* (and were later mentioned by Othello).

89 (3.3.48–9) *Each . . . warrant of*:   'every traveller to distant parts will bring us confirmation of '. In some cases, a traveller could deposit money with a broker before departing, and claim five times that sum if he returned with proof of reaching his distant goal; though he lost the money if he failed to reach that goal.

90 (3.3: S.D. after 52) *Thunder . . . vanishes*:   The wording corresponds to that in F1. This event and the following speech derive partly from Virgil. In Virgil's *Aeneid*, Book 3, Aeneas and his men reach an island where they attempt to eat a meal, but harpies (who prove to be invulnerable) descend on the food, pillaging and defiling it. The harpy Celaeno then denounces the sinful travellers. (Virgil says that harpies 'are birds with girls' countenances and a disgusting outflow from their bellies. Their hands have talons . . . '.)

91 (3.3: S.D. after 82) *He . . . table*:   The wording corresponds to that in F1, except that I have supplied '*depart,*'.

92 (3.3.86–90) *So . . . distractions*:   'Similarly, with an effectively life-like performance and remarkable attentiveness, my inferior agents have performed their various rôles. My great spells operate, and these people, my enemies, are all thoroughly distraught.'

93 (3.3.99) *it . . . trespass*:   (a) 'in a deep (bass) voice, it proclaimed my sin'; (b) 'it sang the bass accompaniment to the song of my sin (the winds providing the higher parts)'.

94 (4.1.3) *a third . . . life*:   His late wife was one third, he another, and Miranda another.

95 (4.1.9) *of her*:   F1 has 'her of ', which may be a compositor's error. Wilson reads 'hereof ', meaning 'of my rich gift'.

96 (4.1.13) *gift*:   F1 has 'guest', which is probably a compositor's misreading.

97 (4.1.13–23) *Then . . . you*:   Anne Hathaway was pregnant when she married William Shakespeare in 1582. It appears that Shakespeare had not practised the abstinence later preached by Prospero.

98 (4.1.28–31) *to take . . . below*:   'to mar the ardour of the celebratory day on which I (impatient for sexual fulfilment) shall think either that the sun-god's horses have collapsed (because time is moving so slowly) or that night is kept underground in chains'. (Phoebus Apollo, the classical sun-god, drove across the sky a chariot pulled by a team of horses.)

99 (4.1.55–6) *The white . . . liver*:   'the purity of my love controls the ardour of my sexual desire'. While the heart was regarded as the source of love and understanding, the liver was regarded as the source of sexual desire and violent passions.

100 (4.1.57–8) *Bring . . . spirit*:   'Bring one too many, rather than lack a spirit (to assist you)'.

101 (4.1: S.D. after 59) Enter IRIS: In the masque which begins here, the parts of Iris, Ceres and Juno are supposedly played by spirits directed by Ariel. Iris is the goddess of the rainbow and a messenger of the gods. Ceres is the goddess of the earth's produce, particularly of cereal crops. Juno, wife of Jupiter, is the goddess of marriage and procreation. The gist of the masque is that Venus and Cupid, who hoped to incite lust in the lovers, have been defeated by the lovers' determination to postpone sexual intercourse until after marriage; and Iris, Ceres and Juno proceed to bless the future wedding.

102 (4.1.64) *banks . . . brims*:   Editors are uncertain of the meaning. One interpretation is: 'banks with edges raised by digging and reinforced by woven supports'. Another, deeming 'pionèd' a variant of 'peonied' and emending 'twillèd' as 'tuliped' or 'lilied', is: 'banks with edges bearing peonies and tulips [or lilies]'.

103 (4.1.68) *pole-clipped vineyard*:   The line's metre is improved if the final word is pronounced trisyllabically, with stress on the first and third syllables: '*vin*-ee-*ard*'. F1 gives the adjective as 'pole-clipt', which some editors treat as 'pole-clipped' (meaning 'with poles embraced by vines') and others as 'poll-clipped' ('with tops pruned', which seems less likely).

104 (4.1: S.D. after 72) *A peacock-drawn . . . descends*:   F1 has the direction '*Iuno descends*'. The dialogue indicates that Juno descends in a chariot supposedly drawn by peacocks (birds sacred to the goddess).

105 (4.1: S.D. after 75) *Enter CERES*: Orgel (p. 175) assumes that Ceres is played by Ariel, but the evidence is unclear.

106 (4.1.88–9) *they . . . got*: Ovid's *Metamorphoses*, Bk. 5, says that when Proserpine (Persephone), daughter of Ceres, was gathering flowers, Dis, god of the underworld, lustfully abducted her to his realm. Venus and Cupid had prompted his desire in order to extend their powers to the underworld. Subsequently, Proserpine was allowed to return to the upper world for part of the year.

107 (4.1.93–4) *Paphos . . . her*: Venus was supposed to have risen from the sea at Paphos, on the coast of Cyprus, and she was worshipped at a temple there. Doves, sacred to Venus, pulled her chariot.

108 (4.1.94–101) *here . . . out*: 'done / Some wanton charm' means 'imposed some lust-inducing sorcery'. '[N]o bed-rite shall be paid / Till Hymen's torch be lighted' means 'no sexual intercourse will take place before marriage'. (F1 has 'bed-right', but the sense is much the same.) 'Mars's hot minion' (Mars's randy darling) is Venus, who was married to Vulcan but committed adultery with Mars. Cupid is 'waspish-headed' because he is often minded to sting (by means of his arrows). Sparrows are traditionally deemed lecherous. '[R]ight out' means 'simply and straightforwardly'.

109 (4.1: S.D. after 105) *JUNO . . . together*: In F1, the song is nominated as Juno's alone, although it is preceded by the direction '*They Sing.*'. Some editors allocate its first four lines to Juno and the last eight to Ceres, but Ferdinand's subsequent comment that the song is charmingly 'harmonious' confirms that Juno and Ceres sing part or all of it together.

110 (4.1.114–15) *Spring . . . harvest!*: 'may spring come to you at the earliest opportunity – immediately after harvest-time (so that there is no winter)!'

111 (4.1.123–4) *So rare . . . Paradise*: Like Adam (son of God) in the Garden of Eden, Ferdinand has a wonderful ('wondered') and wise father. Orgel (p. 178) reads 'wife' for 'wise', explaining that the word in F1 is actually 'wife', though its 'f' has a broken crossbar and may be mistaken for a long 's'. This 'wife', however, is probably a compositor's misreading of an

authorial 'wise', given that 'wise' rhymes with 'Paradise' and that Miranda is not yet Ferdinand's spouse.

112 (4.1.124: S.D.) Juno . . . employment.: I reproduce the wording of the direction in F1.

113 (4.1.124) *Sweet now, silence:*: I reproduce the wording and punctuation of F1. It may mean either 'Be so good as to be silent:' or 'Dear person (Ferdinand), be silent:'.

114 (4.1.128) *windring brooks*: 'meandering brooks'. Some editors, suspecting a misprint, emend F1's 'windring' to 'winding' or 'wand'ring'.

115 (4.1: S.D. after 138) Enter . . . speaks.: In F1, the direction here is: '*Enter certaine Reapers (properly habited:) they ioyne with the Nimphes, in a gracefull dance, towards the end whereof,* Prospero *starts sodainly and speakes, after which to a strange hollow and confused noyse, they heauily vanish.*' The latter part of this direction refers to what happens a few lines later. '[P]roperly', 'hollow' and 'heauily' mean 'appropriately', 'howling' (or 'sepulchral') and 'gloomily'.

116 (4.1.145) *anger so distempered*: 'such extreme anger'. 'Distempered' meant 'with the bodily humours ill-balanced'.

117 (4.1.164) *Come . . . come!*: F1 has 'Come with a thought; I thank thee *Ariell*: come.' This may mean: 'Ariel, come as soon as I, now, think of you. Thank you: I know [or see] that you are on the way. Come on!'. Although 'thee' is singular, some editors assume that 'I thank thee' is uttered towards the departing Ferdinand and Miranda in response to their wish for his peace of mind. Wilson emends 'I thank thee' as 'I think thee' (i.e. 'I'm thinking of you, Ariel').

118 (4.1.167) *when I presented Ceres*: Some editors interpret this as 'when I played the part of Ceres', noting that Ariel, a singer, would be appropriate as the actor of Ceres, who sings. (Iris does not sing.) An alternative interpretation is 'when I organised the masque of Ceres', because Prospero enjoined Ariel to work primarily as manager of the masque. The latter option better fits Ariel's implication that he had been in a position to warn Prospero.

119 (4.1.184) *O'erstunk their feet*:   Although F1 specifies 'feet' (and the notion of smelly feet seems apt here), some editors emend this as 'feat' or 'sweat'.

120 (4.1.220–21) *O King . . . thee!*:   Trinculo's phrasing recalls the ballad (also quoted in *Othello*) which begins:

> King Stephen was and-a worthy peer;
> His breeches cost him but a crown.
> He held them sixpence all too dear;
> With that he called his tailor lown . . .

('Lown' means 'lout'.)

121 (4.1.232) *Make . . . stuff*:   'make us look like peculiar material'.

122 (4.1.234–5) *Now . . . bald jerkin*:   The jerkin is 'under the line' (under, or taken down from, the clothes-line), but the phrase can also mean 'at the equator'; and, in shipboard ceremonies at the crossing of the equator, a mariner might have his head shaved: hence, 'you are like to lose your hair'. A 'bald' jerkin is worn or threadbare. Trinculo proceeds to extend the pun on 'line' by saying that they steal 'by line and level' (by use of the plumb-line and the carpenter's level): properly, thoroughly.

123 (4.1.241) *put . . . fingers*:   'do some stealing yourself'. Bird-lime, a sticky substance, was smeared on twigs to trap birds.

124 (4.1: S.D. after 250) *They . . . on.*:   F1 reads: '*A noyse of Hunters heard. Enter divers Spirits in shape of Dogs and Hounds, hunting them about: Prospero and Ariel setting them on.*'

125 (5.1.2–5) *Time . . . cease*:   'Time / Goes upright with his carriage' means 'Time no longer walks stooping under a heavy burden' (because most of the tasks to be completed in the set time are finished). The reference to 'the sixth hour' (6 p.m.) emphasises not only the chronological confines of the magical action but also the neatness of the dramatic scheme. (F1's spelling, 'hower', shows that 'hour' is disyllabic and the line regular.)

126 (5.1.23–4) *that relish . . . they*:   'being quite as sensitive to suffering as they are'.

127 (5.1.25–8) *Though . . . vengeance*:   Prospero's words echo and

encapsulate part of Montaigne's essay 'Of Crueltie' (*Essayes*, 1603, Bk. 2, Chap. 11), which says:

> He that through a naturall facilitie, & genuine mildnesse, should neglect or contemne injuries received, should no doubt performe a rare action, and worthy commendation: But he who being toucht & stung to the quicke, with any wrong or offence received, should arme himselfe with reason against this furiously-blinde desire of revenge, and in the end after a great conflict, yeeld himselfe master over-it, should doubtlesse doe much more. The first should doe well, the other vertuously: the one action might be termed goodnesse, the other vertue.

128 (5.1: S.D. after 32) *Prospero . . . staff.*: This stage-direction is an inference from F1's later reference to '*the circle which* Prospero *had made*'.

129 (5.1.37–40) *By moonshine . . . curfew*: The 'green sour ring-lets' are fairy rings, circles of darker grass caused by the outward spread of fungus, but supposedly caused by fairies dancing. '[M]ushrumps' are mushrooms. The 'solemn curfew' is the bell that rings at 9 p.m., supposedly a cue for nocturnal spirits.

130 (5.1.41) *(Weak . . . be)*: '(although you are weak ministers)'. *Macbeth*, Act 4, scene 1, shows that, paradoxically, 'masters' could sometimes mean 'ministers' or 'agents'.

131 (5.1.33–50) *Ye elves . . . art*: These lines derive partly from a speech by Medea, the enchantress, in Ovid's *Metamorphoses*, Bk. 7. Medea invokes the spirits which haunt the natural world (with its 'standing lakes') and have aided her manifold sorcery, including the raising of storms and the uprooting of trees. When Prospero says that he has made graves open and release the dead, he is not literally truthful, but his words echo Medea's claim, 'I call up dead men from their graves'. (In line 45, the oak is 'Jove's' because this durable tree is sacred to Jove; his 'bolt' is the thunderbolt.)

132 (5.1: S.D. after 57) *Here . . . speaks.*: The wording here corresponds to that in F1. Ariel is unseen by these castaways, and, until line 106, they are unaware of Prospero's physical presence, though they may partly intuit his meanings.

133 (5.1.58–60) *A solemn . . . skull*: Musical therapy is also employed in *King Lear* and *Pericles*. F1 has 'boile within thy skull': Orgel (p. 191) preserves 'boil', taking it to mean 'which boil'; but editors usually emend it as 'boiled'.

134 (5.1.60–61) *There . . . spell-stopped*: The previous words, using 'thy', referred to Alonso; but here the use of 'you' indicates that he is probably (as my S.D. indicates) addressing Antonio and Sebastian, though he may possibly be addressing Alonso's group as a whole.

135 (5.1.66–8) *their rising . . . reason*: 'their recovering senses begin to expel the fogs of ignorance that cover their gradually-improving minds'.

136 (5.1.70–71) *pay . . . Home*: 'fully reward your kindnesses'.

137 (5.1.96) *So . . . so*: 'Thus, thus, thus': Prospero is guiding Ariel's task of attiring him.

138 (5.1.116–18) *This . . . resign*: 'This situation – if it really exists – demands a most unusual explanatory account. I give up my interest in your usurped dukedom (the homage and payments it brought me)'.

139 (5.1.145–8) *As great . . . daughter*: 'It is as great to me as it is recent; and I have far weaker means than you to make the grievous loss bearable, for I have lost my daughter.' (Marring the ironic truth of his statement, which hinges on 'losing' a daughter to her prospective husband, he implies that Miranda is dead, whereas Claribel, Alonso's married daughter, remains alive.)

140 (5.1.153–7) *these lords . . . breath*: 'these lords are so amazed at this meeting that their reasoning faculties are swallowed up, and they hardly believe that their eyes see truly or that their words are normal utterances'.

141 (5.1.163) *'tis . . . day*: 'the account of events will take several days'.

142 (5.1: S.D. after 171) *Here . . . chess.*: This direction corresponds to that in F1. Presumably Prospero draws aside a curtain which screens the cave-mouth. Here *'discovers'* means 'reveals'.

143 (5.1.174–5) *Yes ... play*:   'On the contrary: you would
        craftily contend with me for twenty kingdoms, which are less
        than the world; but I would still call it fair play (because I
        love you).'

144 (5.1.196) *I am hers*:   'And I am *her* second father.'

145 (5.1.213) *When ... own*:   (a) 'when we had lost our senses';
        (b) 'when we were captives of vice and error'.

146 (5.1: S.D. after 215) Enter ... following.:   This S.D. keeps
        the wording of F1.

147 (5.1.218–20) *Now ... land?*:   'Now, blasphemous fellow,
        in the custom of driving God's grace overboard by your
        swearing, have you no oaths ashore? Are you dumb on land?'

148 (5.1.236) *all our trim*:   'all our garments'. F1 has 'all our
        trim', but some editions emend this as 'all her trim' ('all the
        ship's sails, rigging, etc.').

149 (5.1.240) *brought moping hither*:   'brought here disconso-
        lately'. They are 'moping' because they have suddenly been
        separated from their fine ship and her master. (An alternative
        gloss is 'brought here in a bewildered state'.)

150 (5.1.247–50) *At picked ... accidents*:   'In a chosen time of
        leisure (and soon my leisure will be full-time), I shall provide
        what you will regard as a plausible explanation of every one
        of these incidents which have occurred'. Where F1 has
        '(Which shall be shortly single) I'le resolue you', some editors
        prefer to emend the line as 'Which shall be shortly, single I'll
        resolve you'. In that emendation, 'single' is supposed to mean
        'privately'.

151 (5.1.256–8) *Every ... coragio!*:   In his first sentence, Stephano
        drunkenly reverses the normal exhortation, which would be
        'Every man shift for himself, and let no man take care for all
        the rest'. 'Coragio' (from the Italian *coraggio*) means 'Courage –
        be brave'; and 'bully-monster' means (more or less) 'good old
        monster'.

152 (5.1.268–9) *Mark ... true*:   'Observe the liveries of these
        men, my lords; then tell me if the men are honest.' The
        'badges' may refer to heraldic devices worn by servants to
        show whom they serve, or to the uniforms of such servants.
        (Stephano and Trinculo are wearing stolen outfits.)

153 (5.1.270–72) *one . . . power*: 'a witch so powerful that she could control the moon, ordain the ebbing and flowing of tides, and wield lunar authority in a way that exceeded the planet's own power'. (This reading takes 'without' to mean 'beyond'. Other editions interpret the latter part thus: 'and wield the moon's power without her authorisation'; but that is a more strained version.)

154 (5.1.283–5) *I have . . . fly-blowing*: 'Pickle' can mean both 'predicament' and 'preservative liquor'. Trinculo uses both senses, referring to his immersion in the foul lake. He will not fear 'fly-blowing' because, he implies, he is so thoroughly steeped in the disgusting preservative that his flesh will never tempt the flies that lay their eggs in rotting meat.

155 (5.1.310) *dear-belov'd solemnizèd*: F1 has 'deere-belou'd, sol-emnized', confirming that the last word is here stressed on its second and fourth syllables.

156 (5.1.312) *Every . . . grave*: 'one third of my time will be devoted to reflections on the death that awaits me'.

157 (5.1.316–17) *sail . . . off*: 'such speedy sailing that you will catch up with the distant royal fleet'.

158 (5. Epilogue, S.D.) *spoken by* PROSPERO: The ensuing epilogue appears to combine three layers of meaning. In the first, Prospero incorporates the audience in the fictional action, saying that their co-operation is needed if his return to the mainland and the successful completion of his project are to be accomplished. In the second layer (which emerges strongly at lines 9–13), the actor of the rôle solicits the applause and good will of the audience. In the third layer (which emerges strongly at lines 13–20), it may seem not only that Prospero begs for prayers for divine help and that the actor seeks the spectators' indulgence, but also that the playwright, contemplating retirement, asks the hearers for their intercessionary prayers on his behalf. (The 'prayer' of line 16 may be both his to them and theirs for him.) The epilogue's phrasing occasionally recalls that of the Roman Catholic Mass for the Dead: e.g., 'Release, O Lord, the souls of all the faithful departed from the bonds of their sins. And by the assistance of Thy grace may they escape the sentence of condemnation.'

159 (5. Epilogue, 16–18) *Unless . . . faults:*   The range of meaning includes: (a: from Prospero:) 'unless you pray for divine
help and mercy for me (as, being a magician, I have been a
transgressor)'; (b: from the actor:) 'unless I be rescued by this
plea of mine, which, if it be effectively penetrating, forcefully
elicits your mercy and your forgiveness for all the faults (of
the play)'; and possibly (c: from Shakespeare:) 'unless I be
redeemed by your acts of prayer, which have the capacity to
be so effectively penetrating that they forcefully solicit God,
source of all mercy, and thus obtain my liberation from sin
and error'.

GLOSSARY

Where a pun or an ambiguity is apparent, the meanings are distinguished as (a) and (b), or (a), (b) and (c), etc. Otherwise, alternative meanings are distinguished as (i) and (ii), or as (i), (ii) and (iii), etc. Abbreviations include the following: adj., adjective; adv., adverb; esp., especially; *O.E.D.*, *Oxford English Dictionary*; vb., verb.

a-batfowling: go a-batfowling:
2.1.178: (a) go about killing birds at night; (b) set out to fool a gullible victim.

abroad: 5.1.167: beyond.

abuse: 5.1.112: delude.

abysm: abyss.

accidents: occurrences.

achès: 1.2.371: aches. (When a noun, 'aches' was pronounced 'aitches'; when a verb, 'aiks'.)

admire: wonder.

advance: 1.2.412, 4.1.177: raise.

affections: 5.1.18: emotions.

after: 5.1.92: pursuing.

against an oracle: 4.1.12: even if an oracle denies it.

agèd cramps: cramps of old age.

ague: feverish illness.

airs: songs, melodies.

airy: 5.1.54: (a) in the air; (b) using music.

amazement: 1.2.14: dismay.

an: 2.1.174: if.

and if: 2.2.112, 5.1.117: if.

anger so distempered: 4.1.145: (a) such extreme anger; (b, as 'anger, so distempered':) anger and so troubled.

angle: 1.2.223: corner.

Argier: Algiers.

art: (i: 1.2.1 and later:) magic; (ii: 1.2.25:) accessories of magic.

aspersion: 4.1.18: (a) shower; (b) dew.

as they: 4.1.178: as if they.

attached: seized, arrested.

austerely: rigorously.

avoid: depart, quit.

aye: for aye: for ever.

backward: 1.2.50: past.

bade: ordered.

badge: 5.1.268: (a) servant's livery; (b) heraldic device on a servant's livery.

bands: bonds, bindings.

barnacles: 4.1.244: (a) kind of wild goose; (b) small marine crustaceans.

bark: barque: small sailing-ship.

bass my trespass: sing out my guilt in a bass register.

bate: 2.1.96: (a) except; (b) cease to mention; **bate me**: 1.2.250: deduct from my time.

beak: prow.

bear me: conduct myself.

bear off: 2.2.18: keep off.

beating: 4.1.163: (a) throbbing; (b) agitated; **beating on**: 5.1.246: worrying about.

bending: 4.1.174: aiming.

Bermoothès: Bermudas.

betid to: befallen.

betrims: adorns with flowers.

blind: 4.1.90: blindfolded.

blow: 3.1.63: lay eggs in.

boatswain, bosun: foreman of the crew.

boded me: predicted for me.

bolt (noun): thunderbolt.

bombard: 'leather jug or bottle for liquor' (*O.E.D.*).

bootless inquisition: fruitless enquiry.

boresprit: (old form of) bowsprit.

bosky: adorned with bushes and thickets.

bosun: *see* boatswain.

bourn, bound of land: boundaries, landmarks.

bow (noun): 4.1.86: rainbow.

brace (noun): pair.

brave: fine, splendid, beautiful.

broom-groves: thickets of gorse.

burthen: burden.

busil'est: most busily.

butt: 1.2.146: (a) barrel or tub; (b) leaky vessel.

but then: 1.2.503: (a) until then; (b) but therefore.

by and by: after a while.

By'r lakin: By the Virgin Mary.

by what?: 1.2.42: about what?

Caliban: (perhaps) 'Darkness' (from Romany *kauloben*: 'black').

can: 4.1.27: can make.

candied: 2.1.273: turned to sugary confections.

canker (noun): 1.2.419: (a) cancer; (b) spreading disease.

cankers (vb.): 4.1.192: corrupts.

capable of: susceptible to.

carriage: burden carried.

case: in case: 3.2.24: in fit state.

cast: 2.1.244: cast up.

cat o'mountain: wildcat.

Ceres: goddess of nature's bounty, esp. cereal crops.

certes: certainly.

changed eyes: exchanged loving looks.

channel: stream.

Chanticleer: male fowl.

chaps: 2.2.83: chops, jaws; hence, mouth.

charge: responsibility.

charmingly: 4.1.119: (a) entrancingly; (b) magically; (c) melodiously (from Latin *carmen*, song).

charms (noun): spells.

cherubin (plural used as singular): angel.

chick: (term of endearment:) dear little person.

chirurgeonly: like a surgeon.

chough: jackdaw.

clapped: 5.1.231: confined.

clear: 3.3.82: virtuous.

cleave: 4.1.165: adhere.

clock: tell the clock to: agree that it is time for.

closeness: privacy.

coil: tumult, uproar.

cold: 4.1.66: chaste.

common: **in common**: for communal use.

complexion: 1.1.27: character as indicated by facial appearance.

conceive: understand.

condition: situation, position.

conduct (noun): director.

content: 2.1.263: desire, liking.

control: 1.2.443: refute.

coragio (from Italian *coraggio*): (take) courage.

corollary: supernumerary.

couch (vb.): 5.1.90: (a) recline; (b) sleep.

country footing: rustic dancing.

course: **set her two courses**: use both foresail and mainsail.

cout (vb.): (apparently) befool or cheat.

crabs: 2.2.161: (a) crab-apples; (b) the crustaceans.

crack (vb.): 5.1.2: fail suddenly.

cramps: **old cramps**: cramps of old age.

crave: demand, call for.

creature: (i: 1.2.82:) dependant; (ii: 3.1.48:) created being.

credit: **want credit**: lack credibility.

cried: 2.1.313: called out.

crisp: 4.1.130: rippling.

cubit: a variable measure, but often about 20 inches (50 cms.).

Cupid: boyish love-god, son of Venus.

dalliance: amorous behaviour.

dam: mother.

decked: adorned.

delicate: (i: 1.2.272:) sensitive; (ii: 1.2.445, 4.1.49: a) dainty;

(b) ingenious; (iii: 2.1.41:) pleasant; (iv: 2.2.86) exquisitely made.

deliver: 5.1.314: report.

demi-puppets: 5.1.36: (i) beings partly controlled by Prospero's will; (ii) diminutive beings.

dewlapped: with pendulous jowls.

diligent: attentive.

Dis: ruler of the Underworld.

discase me: change my clothes.

discharge (noun): performance.

distempered: unbalanced, extreme.

distinctly: 2.1.210: meaningfully.

ditty: short poem to be sung.

Do, do!: 4.1.236: 'Yes, go on!'

dock: weed with large leaves.

doit: coin of very low value.

dowl: filament of a feather.

down: 4.1.81: open upland.

drift of my purpose: import of my plan.

drollery: **living drollery**: 3.3.21: (a) real-life comedy; (b) living caricature; (c) puppet show with live actors.

dry convulsions: (perhaps) spasms suffered by old people.

dulling: **to the dulling of my spirits**: so that my spirits are dulled.

dusky: 4.1.89: (a) from the region of darkness; (b) gloomy.

earth: 1.2.315: low, primitive creature.

earthed: buried.

eaves of reeds: overhanging ends of thatched roofs.

ebb: **at ebb**: ceasing to flow.

ecstasy: madness.

edge: 4.1.29: ardour.

eld'st: longest.

elements: earth, water, air and fire.

ending: 5. Epilogue, 15: (a) final
    emotion here; (b) deathbed
    emotion.
engine: weapon.
entertainment: treatment.
ere: **or ere**: before.
estate (vb.): bestow.
event: outcome.
every: 5.1.249: every one of.
eye: **an eye of green**: (a) a tinge of
    green; (b) a naïve observer.
exeunt: they go out.
exit: he or she goes out.
extirpate: 1.2.125: (a) uproot;
    (b) expel.
fancy: imagination.
fathom: depth of six feet (about
    180 cm.).
fearful: 1.2.472: (a) cowardly;
    (b) frightening.
feater: neater.
featly: neatly, elegantly.
fellow: 3.1.84: partner.
fetch off: 4.1.212: (a) rescue;
    (b) drink up.
filberts: hazelnuts.
fine: 5.1.262: splendidly dressed.
firing: firewood.
flamed amazement: 1.2.198: 'by
    my flames, induced panic'.
flat-long: with the flat of the blade;
    hence, harmlessly.
flats: marshes.
flatterer: **for my flatterer**: as my
    flatterer.
flesh-fly: blow-fly.
flote: sea.
flout: mock.
fly him: flee from him.
foil: **put it to the foil**: 3.1.46:
    (a) offset it; (b) overthrew it;
    (c) challenged it.

foison: plenty, abundant produce.
foretold you: told you previously.
forthrights and meanders: paths
    variously straight and winding.
foundered: lamed.
fowl weather: 2.1.138: (punning
    on 'foul':) weather according to
    the 'old cock', Gonzalo.
fraughting: forming the cargo.
freshes: **quick freshes**: flowing
    streams of fresh water.
frippery: shop selling old clothes.
from: 1.2.65: outside.
frustrate (adj.): futile.
full poor: very austere.
furze: **brown furze**: dried-up gorse.
gaberdine: loose smock of coarse
    cloth.
gallant (noun): fine young
    gentleman.
garners (noun): granaries.
gave out: declared.
genius: **worser genius**: bad angel,
    evil spirit.
gentle: civilised; **gentle-kind**:
    civilised.
gentleness: kindness, nobility.
gently: graciously.
ghastly: aghast, fearful.
gilded: reddened.
glass: (i: 1.2.240, 5.1.223:) hour-
    glass; (ii: 3.1.50:) mirror; **two
    glasses** (past noon): two o'clock
    in the afternoon.
glut (vb.): swallow.
go: 3.2.18: walk.
got: 1.2.320: begotten.
hag-seed: offspring of a hag.
halt (vb.): limp.
heath: **long heath**: 1.1.61:
    (a) heather; (b) barren heath-land.
heaviness: 5.1.200: grief, sorrow.

hest: behest, command.

high-day: holiday.

hint: occasion.

hoist: 1.2.148: (a) lowered;
(b) launched (*O.E.D.*).

hollow: 4.1.S.D.: (perhaps: a)
howling; (b) sepulchral.

holp: helped.

hoodwink: render harmless.

Hymen's lamps: torches carried at
weddings, Hymen being the
Greek god of marriage.

impertinent: irrelevant.

inch-meal: inch by inch.

Inde: the West Indies.

indulgence: 5. Epilogue, 20:
(a) forgiveness; (b) ecclesiastical
indulgence which remits a
punishment for sin.

influence: 1.2.182: astrological
power.

instrument: **to instrument**: 3.3.54:
(a) as its instrument; (b) in its
control.

invest: 2.1.219: clothe.

Iris: goddess of the rainbow.

issue: offspring.

issued: 1.2.59: descended.

it (possessive adj.): 2.1.158: its.

Jack: **played the Jack with**: made
a fool of.

Jove: Jupiter, the supreme Roman
deity.

justify: prove.

justle: jostle.

keepers: 3.3.20: guardian angels.

kernels: pips.

key: 1.2.83: (a) key of office;
(b) key in musical notation.

kibe: 2.1.270: (a) sore; (b) chilblain.

knot: **sad knot**: folded (arms), a
sign of grief.

lass-lorn: deprived of his young
woman.

late: 5.1.145: recent.

laughter: 2.1.32: (a) number of
eggs laid in one sequence by a
fowl; (b) outburst of mirth.

lays it on: 3.2.145: plays vigorously.

lay-to: 4.1.246: apply.

league: a vaguely-defined distance,
but often three miles.

learning me: teaching me.

leas: meadows.

letters: 2.1.146: (a) literature;
(b) writing; (c) erudition.

lie: 3.2.18: (a) tell lies; (b) lie down.
Give me the lie: call me a liar.

lieu: **in lieu of**: in return for.

life: **with good life**: convincingly.

like: (i: 3.3.66:) equally;
(ii: 5.1.266:) likely.

line: (i.: 4.1.193): (a) clothes-line;
(b, less likely:) lime-tree;
(ii: 4.1.234: a) clothes-line;
(b) equator; (iii: 4.1.236): plumb-
line. **By line and level**:
properly, methodically.

line-grove: grove of lime-trees.

list (vb.): wish.

litter (vb.): give (animal) birth to.

liver: (supposedly) source of sexual
desire and violent passion.

loathly: loathsome.

long heath, brown furze: heather
and dry gorse.

lorded: turned into a lord.

luggage: (i: 4.1.229: a) encum-
brances; (b) pickings;
(ii: 5.1.299:) stolen clothing.

maid: (i: 1.2.431-2: a) unmarried
young woman; (b) virgin;
(ii: 3.1.84: a) maidservant;
(b) virgin.

main-course: mainsail.

make a man: make a man's fortune.

mallow: weed with soft downy leaves.

man: **make a man**: enrich a man.

manage: management, adminis-tration.

manners: behaviour, conduct.

mantled: scum-covered.

mark (vb.): note, pay attention to.

marmoset: small monkey (said to be edible).

massy: heavy.

meaner: lesser.

measure us: traverse us.

meddle with: 1.2.22: (a) engage; (b) intrude upon.

merchant: 2.1.5: (i) mercantile ship; (ii) owner of the cargo.

merely: 1.1.52: completely.

mettle: 2.1.175: (a) spirit; (b) metal.

mid-season: noon.

Millaine: Milan.

mill-wheels strike: 'blades of mill-wheels strike the water'.

mind (vb.): notice.

minion: lover.

ministers: agents.

Miranda: 'Wonderful', 'Admirable'.

miss: 1.2.312: do without.

mistress: 3.1.86: here, 'woman who has command over a man's heart' (*O.E.D.*), not a sexual partner.

mo: more.

monster: grotesque or abnormal creature.

monstrous: (i: 3.2.27: a) enormous; (b) typical of a monster; (ii: 3.3.95:) appallingly strange.

moon-calf: 2.2.102: deformed offspring, monstrosity.

mop: grimace.

moping: 5.1.240: (a) disconsolately; (b) dazedly.

morsel: 2.1.280: (a) choice dish; (b) fragment.

mountaineers: mountain-dwellers.

moved: 4.1.146: disturbed.

mow (noun): derisory grimace.

mum: silence.

murrain: plague.

muse (vb.): wonder, marvel.

mushrump: mushroom.

Naiad: nymph of streams and rivers.

Naples: 1.2.437: the King of Naples.

natural: born fool.

neat's-leather: cow-hide.

Neptune: 5.1.35: (a) Roman trident-wielding sea-god; (b) the sea.

nerves: sinews.

ninny: **pied ninny**: idiot in jester's motley.

Nobody: **picture of Nobody**: invisible person.

nonpareil: paragon.

note (noun): 2.1.241: information.

nymph: (i: 4.1.66: a) rural virgin; (b) virginal rural spirit; (ii: 4.1.128:) virginal rural spirit.

observation strange: remarkable diligence.

o'er ears: drowned.

off and on: 3.2.13: (a) intermit-tently; (b) one way and another.

omit: 1.2.183: disregard.

on: 4.1.157: of.

or ere: before.

out three: fully three.

over-topping: outstripping, going too far.

owe: own.

own (vb.): 5.1.276: acknowledge.

pageant: theatrical performance or display.

pains: 1.2.242: onerous tasks.

Paradise: the Garden of Eden.

pard or cat o' mountain: leopard.

party: person specified.

pass of pate: thrust of wit.

passion: 1.2.396: suffering.

patch (noun): jester, clown.

paunch him: stab him in the belly.

pay . . . home: reward . . . fully.

penetrate: 1.2.288: arouse sympathy in.

perdition: loss.

perfected: 1.2.79: master of the art of.

perforce: necessarily.

pertly: briskly.

phoenix: mythical Arabian bird: only one was supposed to exist at any time.

picked: selected.

pickle: 5.1.282–3: (a) predicament; (b) preservative liquor.

pied: in jester's particoloured costume.

pig-nuts: edible tubers.

pionèd and twillèd: (perhaps) raised by diggers and reinforced.

piteous: pitying.

plantation of: 2.1.139: responsibility for (a) the colonisation of, (b) planting crops on.

play me false: trick me.

play the Jack with: make a fool of.

play the men: (perhaps) act like men.

plume (noun): plumage.

plummet: sounding-line.

pocket up: 2.1.64: (a) conceal; (b) suppress.

point: to point: in exact detail.

pole-clipped: 4.1.68: (a) with poles entwined by vines; (b, as 'poll-clipped':) pruned.

poor-John: dried, salted fish.

post (noun): messenger.

Praise in departing: 'Keep your praise until the end.'

premises: stipulations.

presently: immediately.

prize (noun): booty.

probable: plausible.

professes: 2.1.229: makes it his profession.

project: 2.1.293; 5. Epilogue, 12: (a) plan; (b) purpose.

properly: 4.1.S.D.: appropriately.

proper selves: very selves.

Prospero: 'Fortunate', 'Prosperous'.

provision: foresight.

purchased: **worthily purchased**: 4.1.14: (a) fully paid for; (b) nobly gained.

putter-out: gambler.

quaint: 1.2.318: (a) ingenious; (b) strangely distinctive. **Quaint device**: ingenious mechanism.

quality: 1.2.193: (a) fraternity; (b) talents.

Queen of state: majestic Queen.

quickens: enlivens, revives.

rabble: 4.1.37: troupe of minor spirits.

race: 'natural or inherited disposition' (*O.E.D.*).

rack: 4.1.156: (a) wisp of cloud; (b) wind-driven cloud or mist.

rapt in: engrossed in.

rate: estimation.

reason: do reason: do anything reasonable.

recover: cure.

red plague: (perhaps) bubonic plague.

reeling-ripe: so drunk as to be about to reel.

rein: **give . . . the rein**: allow . . . freedom.

relation: 5.1.164: story.

remember: 1.2.409: commemorate.

revels: entertainments.

rid: 1.2.365: destroy.

rifted: split.

roarers: stormy seas.

rounded with: 4.1.158: (a) rounded off by, completed by; (b) surrounded by.

run: 3.2.17: flee from the foe.

sack: white wine.

salvage (noun): savage.

sanctimonious: sacred.

sans (from French): without.

save: 2.1.49: except.

scamel: (perhaps) kind of small fish.

scandalled: scandalous, notorious.

scape: escape.

scout (vb.): mock.

screen: barrier.

sea-marge: sea-shore.

sedged crowns: crowns or wreaths of reeds.

set: 3.2.8-9: (a) staring vacantly; (b) located.

Setebos: reputedly a 'great devil' of the Patagonians.

several: diverse.

shake: 2.2.81: shake off.

shift (vb.): make do, improvise.

sicklemen: reapers.

siege: excrement, turd.

signiory: city-state.

single: 5.1.248: (probably) continuous.

sir: 5.1.69: gentleman.

sirrah: (contemptuous form of address:) little man.

skilless: ignorant.

smell: 4.1.198: stink of.

sociable to the show: sympathetic to the display.

something (adv.): somewhat.

sore: (i: 3.1.11:) harsh; (ii: 5.1.289: a) sorry, inept; (b) in pain.

sort: 4.1.146: condition, state; **in a sort**: comparatively speaking.

sot: fool.

south-west (noun): supposedly an unhealthy wind.

spies: 5.1.259: eyes.

spurs: roots.

stale (noun): decoy, bait.

standard: 3.2.15-16: (a) standard-bearer; (b) person standing upright.

stand to: set to, begin eating.

steaded: been useful.

still: 4.1.108, 5.1.214: constantly.

still-vexed: 1.2.229: constantly troubled (by storms).

stockfish: dried cod or hake, beaten before cooking.

stover: hay for winter fodder.

strangely: remarkably; **take the ear strangely**: sound remarkably interesting.

study of: scrutinise.

sty (vb.): confine as a pig in a sty.

subtle: (i: 2.1.41:) gentle; (ii: 2.1.44:) crafty..

succession: inheritance.

suffered: 1.2.231: undergone.

suggestion: 2.1.282: prompting to evil.

suits: 1.2.79: appeals, requests.

sulphurous: explosive (as gunpowder was made from sulphur).

sustaining garments: clothing which helps people to float.

swabber: seaman who cleans decks.

sway (noun): power.

Sycorax: (perhaps) 'Nasty Old Crow'. (See note to 1.2.258-9).

tabor: small drum.

taborer: drummer.

tang: sting.

taste some subtleties: experience some subtle enchantments.

teen: 1.2.64: (a) trouble; (b) grief.

tell: 2.1.15: count.

temperance: 2.1.41-3: (a) mildness of climate; (b, as 'Temperance') name of a woman.

tempered: compounded and hardened.

temple: 1.2.461: sacred place; hence, divine form.

tend: pay attention.

tender (vb.): (i: 2.1.264:) regard; (ii: 4.1.5:) offer.

then: 1.2.503: (a) therefore; (b) until then.

three glasses since: three hours ago.

throes (vb.): pangs.

throughly: thoroughly.

tight and yare: watertight and seaworthy.

tilth: tillage, cultivation of crops.

time: 2.1.296: opportunity; **when time was**: once upon a time.

to: 2.1.70: for.

topsail: sail which extends across the topmast.

touch (noun): sense.

traffic: commerce, trade.

trash (vb.): restrain.

travail: 3.3.15: (a) travel; (b) laborious exertion.

trenchering: trenchers (wooden dishes).

trice: **on a trice**: in an instant.

trick: rapid feat.

tricksy: 5.1.226: (a) playful; (b) ingenious.

trifle (noun): insubstantial entity.

trifling: mere equivocation.

trim (noun): gear, clothing.

trim (vb.): prepare, tidy.

Trinculo (from Italian *trincare* and *culo*): 'Booze-Bum'.

troll the catch: sing the round.

troops: 1.2.220: groups.

trumpery: attractive rubbish.

try with main-course: come close into the wind by using the mainsail.

twillèd: 4.1.64: (perhaps: a) plaited as reinforcement; or (b) ridged, raised.

twink: **with a twink**: in the twinkling (duration of a wink) of an eye.

unbacked: unridden.

undergoing stomach: stoical capacity; courage to endure.

uneasy: 1.2.455: (a) troubled; (b) difficult.

unshrubbed down: bare upland.

unstaunched wench: common woman who (probably) is freely menstruating.

up-staring: standing on end.

urchins: 1.2.327: (a) hedgehogs; (b) sprites or goblins in the form of hedgehogs; (c) goblins. **Urchin-shows**: apparitions of hedgehogs.

use of service: employment of servants.

vanity: 4.1.41: trivial entertainment.

varlets: 4.1.170: (a) servants, menials; (b) low rogues.

vast of night: desolate period of deep night.

veins o'th' earth: 1.2.255:
  (a) seams of minerals;
  (b) underground streams.
vent (vb.): excrete.
verdure: 1.2.87: vitality; hence,
  power.
verily: in truth, truly.
vetches: pea-like plants grown for
  fodder.
viands: food.
virgin-knot: hymen.
vision: 5.1.176: illusion.
visitation: 3.1.32: visit.
visitor: comforter of needy people.
vouched: alleged, affirmed.
vouchsafe: grant.
waist: **in the waist**: amidships.
waits upon: 1.2.392: attends, serves.
waking: 2.1.202: awake.
wallets of flesh: dangling jowls.
want: lack.
ward: 1.2.475: defensive posture.
waspish-headed: minded to sting.
waste: 5.1.303: occupy, pass.
weather-fends: protects from the
  weather.
weeds: 4.1.21: (a) garden weeds;
  (b) bad results.
weep: 3.1.19: imitate weeping by
  exuding resin.
weighed: 2.1.126: (a) pondered;
  (b) balanced.
welkin: sky.

wench: young woman.
wet the grief on't: weep over the
  sorrow of it.
wezand (weasand): throat, gullet.
whelp: pup, cub.
while-ere: **but while-ere**: just a
  short time ago.
whist: 1.2.379: stilled.
whoreson (adj.): no better than the
  son of a whore.
wide-chopped: big-mouthed.
windring: winding, meandering.
wink: (i: 2.1.209:) close the eyes;
  (ii: 2.1.235:) glimpse;
  (iii: 2.1.279:) sleep. **The perpetual wink**: everlasting sleep:
  death.
without: 5.1.272: (a) without;
  (b) beyond.
wondered (adj.): 4.1.123: wonderful.
works (vb.): 4.1.144: agitates.
wound with: entwined by.
wrack (noun): wreck; **wracked**
  (vb.): wrecked.
wrangle: contend.
yard: spar bearing a sail.
yare: (i: 1.1.5: a) prompt;
  (b) skilful; (ii: 5.1.224: a) trim;
  (b) seaworthy.
yarely: 1.1.3: (a) promptly;
  (b) skilfully.
zenith: 1.2.181: best chance of
  success.